BLACK✦STARS
OF COLONIAL AND
REVOLUTIONARY TIMES

BLACK✦STARS
OF COLONIAL AND
REVOLUTIONARY TIMES

✦

written by

JIM HASKINS
CLINTON COX
BRENDA WILKINSON

JIM HASKINS, GENERAL EDITOR

John Wiley & Sons, Inc.

Copyright © 2002 by Jim Haskins. All rights reserved
Published by John Wiley & Sons, Inc., Hoboken, New Jersey
Published simultaneously in Canada

Design and production by Navta Associates, Inc.

For general information about our other products and services, please contact our
Customer Care Department within the United States at (800) 762-2974, outside the
United States at (317) 572-3993 or fax (317) 572-4002.

Wiley also publishes its books in a variety of electronic formats. Some content that
appears in print may not be available in electronic books.

ISBN 0-471-21151-6

Printed in the United States of America

10 9 8 7 6 5 4 3 2 1

Contents

Acknowledgments,   *vii*

Introduction,   *1*

Estevanico,   3

Anthony Johnson,   9

Crispus Attucks,   13

Benjamin Banneker,   18

Marie-Thérèse Metoyer,   24

Jean Baptiste Point du Sable,   29

Private Peter Salem,   35

Private Austin Dabney,   39

Phillis Wheatley,   42

Private Lemuel Haynes,   49

Paul Cuffe,   54

Richard Allen,   59

James Forten,   65

Deborah Sampson,   69

Dr. James Derham,   74

Pierre Toussaint,   79

"Free Frank" McWorter,   83

Catherine (Katy) Ferguson,   89

Daniel Coker,   93

Chronology,   *99*

Notes,   *101*

Bibliography,   *103*

Picture Credits,   *105*

Author Credits,   *107*

Index,   *109*

ACKNOWLEDGMENTS

Thanks to Kathy Benson for her help.

BLACK✦STARS
OF COLONIAL AND
REVOLUTIONARY TIMES

INTRODUCTION

✦

The largest single group of non–English-speaking people to arrive in the North American colonies before the Revolutionary War were African slaves. Never again has the proportion of blacks to whites been as high as during the eighteenth century. Blacks were as pioneering as the Europeans and came as explorers and colonizers as well as builders of the New World.

African slavery in the colonies did not become firmly established until late in the 1600s. Until that time, the lines between slave and free—and between black, white, and Indian—were not clearly drawn. Only after the colonies began to grow and attract a greater population was a large slave labor force established.

Slavery differed from one colony to another. On the eastern coast of North America, for example, the climate in the northern regions did not support extensive farming. Slavery there tended to be "family slavery," with a few slaves living and working side by side with small farmers or craftsmen. In the South where fertile land and warm climates made large-scale cultivation possible, plantation slavery developed. Large numbers of slaves lived and worked far distant from their owners.

From earliest times, a few slaves managed to learn to read and write or prosper at trades. Some seized their own freedom by running away or by arranging to purchase themselves; others made a conscious choice to remain with their owners. Some became slave owners themselves. Others campaigned for an end to slavery. Over time, the majority of Americans of African heritage set down deep psychological roots in the soil of their new land. They took to heart the assertions of the right of individual freedom that were so much a part of the American colonial and Revolutionary eras. Many fought in the War of Independence, some for the British, who promised them freedom in return.

After the American colonies secured their independence from Great Britain, black Americans hoped that the same leaders who had yearned for their own freedom would end slavery. Although such hopes proved futile, the turmoil of the Revolutionary era produced a new people—African Americans. Enslaved or free, they formed their own self-help organizations and religious institutions and helped create the social and cultural life of the new nation. As the United States began to shape itself as a new entity, African Americans continued to play a significant role.

The people who are profiled in the following pages represent the many ways that African Americans played significant roles in American life early and established the groundwork for the important contributions to follow.

ESTEVANICO

(?–1539)

Before European colonization, blacks were among the earliest explorers of the New World. Accompanying various English, Spanish, and French expeditions as sailors and navigators, they made significant contributions to European knowledge of previously unknown lands. Blacks traveled with Columbus on his expeditions to the New World. Thirty blacks accompanied Vasco Nuñez de Balboa, who is regarded as the first European to see (and stand in the waters of) the eastern shore of the Pacific Ocean, in 1513. Although the names of most of those early black explorers are lost to history, one name has come down: Stephan Dorantez, known as Estevanico, who was one of the earliest explorers of what is now the western United States.

Dorantez, also known as "Little Stephen" and Esteban, was born in the port city of Azemmour, Morocco, in about 1503. When he was ten years old, Portuguese invaders captured Azemmour and used it as a base of operations for its voyages further down the western coast of Africa. A great drought occurred ten years later, and Estevanico was among the many Moroccans sold into slavery in Europe.

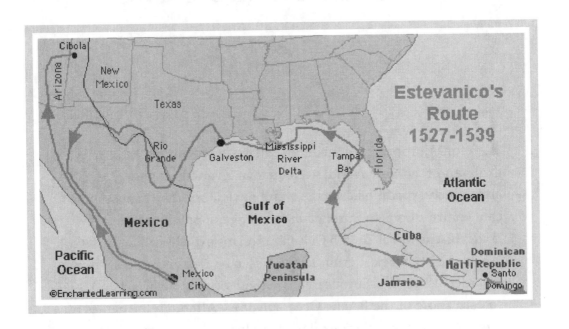

Estevanico became the personal servant of Andres de Dorantes of Bejar del Castanar of old Castile. Dorantes was commander of a company of infantry in an expedition being formed by Pánfilo de Narváez to explore and conquer the lands stretching west from Florida along the Gulf of Mexico. Narváez had spent more than twenty years as a *conquistador* in Mexico. He had received a royal appointment as Spain's governor in Florida and was eager to take control of his new territory, explore it, and begin exploiting its wealth. The 600-man expedition boarded four ships at Sanlúcar de Barrameda, Spain, on June 17, 1527, and set off on a long and difficult sea voyage.

Bad luck plagued the expedition almost from the beginning. When the ships landed at the Caribbean island of Santo Domingo to take on water and food, 143 men deserted. More men were lost in a hurricane that struck the expedition as it proceeded to Cuba. The hurricane also destroyed one of Narváez's ships and damaged the others, forcing the party to winter in Cuba. When they set out again in February 1528, they had to weather still more violent storms before reaching Florida. It was mid-April when the four original ships and a brigantine purchased to replace the vessel that had been lost dropped anchor just north of Tampa Bay on the western coast of Florida. Some 400 men remained, along with 42 horses.

As the explorers made their way upland, many became ill. Florida Indians attacked the party, killing most of them. The survivors were desperate to get away from Florida. Thinking that the Mexican coast lay across the Gulf of Mexico, they toiled for six weeks to make crude barges. On September 22, 1528, they sailed west. As they approached land, the boats capsized. By the time they reached the Texas coast near Galveston, only about 80 remained.

The local Indians were friendly at first. But without warning they enslaved the newcomers. After five years of hard work and exposure to disease, only four of the original expedition survived. They were Estevanico, Dorantes, Alvar Nuñez Cabeza de Vaca, and Alonso

Castillo. In 1534, the four escaped inland and met up with another Indian who judged by their unusual appearance that they must possess magical powers. Asked by one Indian to cure a severe headache, Alonso Castillo made the sign of the cross over him and asked God to heal him, and immediately the Indian said that all the pain was gone. The travelers took well to their new role as medicine men, applying their own knowledge to the lore the Indians taught them. Free to go wherever they wished, the four decided to continue west and hoped to reach Mexico.

Estevanico proved especially gifted in languages, and became fluent in several Indian dialects. He carried a medicine rattle—a feathered, beaded gourd given to him by a chief—as his good luck symbol and trademark. Alvar Nunez Cabeza de Vaca, who later wrote a book about his experiences, told how Estevanico employed his skills as a linguist to help his fellow travelers. His facility with languages enabled him to communicate with the Indians they met along the way and to learn about the geography ahead: where there were settlements, which Indian tribes were hostile or friendly. Cabeza de Vaca wrote that Estevanico "was our go-between; he informed himself about the ways we wished to take, what towns there were, and the matters we desired to know." In spite of his leadership role, Estevanico remained the slave of his master.

The four traveled from the Galveston area west through Texas, up the Rio Grande, through Presidio. Because they traveled east to west,

AFRICANS IN THE NEW WORLD

Estevanico and his comrades may have dressed like Quetzalcoatl, the feathered serpent of ancient Mexican mythology. Some scholars believe that the idea of a giant feathered serpent may have been brought to Central America from Africa.

they became known as "The Children of the Sun." Crossing into Mexico near El Paso, they arrived at San Miguel de Culiacan, a small Spanish outpost in Sinaloa, Mexico, in May 1536. From there they traveled to Mexico City, arriving in July.

During his travels, Estevanico had heard from the Indians legends about a land called Cibola and its Seven Cities of Gold. This story caught the imagination of the viceroy of Mexico, Antonio de Mendoza, who asked the travelers to lead an expedition back into Arizona and New Mexico. Only Estevanico agreed to go. Either purchased from or leased by his owner to Mendoza, he served as scout to a party commanded by a Franciscan priest named Fray Marcos de Niza, which set out on foot northward in February 1539. Estevanico went in advance of the party, sending runners back daily. It had been prearranged that the runners would carry crosses to indicate what lay ahead. A small cross meant a small village, a big cross a larger settlement.

Eventually, Estevanico arrived in northwest New Mexico and saw a large village with buildings constructed of stone several tiers high. This was Hawikuh, a Zuñi pueblo. Apparently certain that he had found Cibola and at least one of its Seven Cities of Gold, he immediately sent a runner back to Fray Marcos with a huge cross. Then he approached the pueblo. But the medicine gourd that had brought him good luck in the past did not have the expected effect on the Zuñi. It was trimmed with the feathers of an owl, a bird that symbolized death to the Zuñi. Estevanico was placed under "house arrest" while the village elders decided his fate. The next morning, he was attacked and killed by Zuñi warriors.

Without his scout, Fray Marcos could not go on. He returned to Mexico, the expedition a failure. The legend of Cibola and the Seven Cities of Gold persists to this day. Another legend arose in southwestern Indian lore about a black "Mexican" who traveled among the Indians long ago.

No one knows where Estevanico is buried. Hawikuh itself no longer exists, having been abandoned in 1670 after a series of wars that the Zuñis fought against the Spaniards and the Apache. A bust of Estevanico, modeled on the visage of a handsome black man, is included in the Twelve Travelers monument in the city of El Paso, Texas.

ANTHONY
JOHNSON
(?–1670)

In the early colonial days, blacks from Africa were not the only people to be bought and sold. Native American Indians could be enslaved. White Europeans were often indentured servants, bound to work for a master for a specified number of years. Slavery and servitude were not closely identified with race. In those early times, blacks had many opportunities to secure their freedom by escaping or buying themselves out of slavery, and once free they had a good chance to make their success in the new land. The life of Anthony Johnson illustrates the possibilities for blacks in the early period of European colonization in North America.

Johnson's existence is first documented in 1621, when a slave known as "Antonio, a Negro" was sold to the English at Jamestown. He went to work for a family named Bennett, who commended him for his "hard labor and known service." He was permitted to wed a fellow slave named Mary and to baptize his children. Eventually securing his freedom, he took the name Anthony Johnson. He

remained close to the Bennetts, however, and when they moved across the Chesapeake Bay to the eastern shore of Virginia, he followed.

In Virginia, the Johnson family established their own farm, where they grew tobacco and corn. Like other planters in the region, Johnson needed help to run his farm. He sponsored slaves entering the colony, and the colonial government granted him 250 acres of land in return. When his farm burned in 1653, the government agreed to reduce his taxes so he could rebuild.

The year following the fire, one of Johnson's slaves, John Casar, ran away to a neighboring farm. Johnson went to court to get his slave back. The legal proceedings took a year, but eventually Johnson won his case.

In 1665, Anthony and Mary Johnson moved to Somerset County, Maryland, where the land was richer. They established a 300-acre farm called Tonies Vineyard. Johnson deeded fifty of his acres back in Virginia to his son, Richard. He sold the other 200 acres to two white planters, who promised to pay him in tobacco. Two years later, according to the agreement of sale, planter Edmund Scarburgh delivered 1,344 pounds of tobacco to the Somerset County sheriff as payment for Johnson's land.

But Scarburgh had no real intention of giving up his tobacco crop. By the 1660s, slavery and servitude had become more closely identified with dark skin, and the colonial legal system had begun to preserve the rights of whites and to deprive blacks of theirs. It was much easier for dishonest whites to get away with cheating blacks. Scarburgh forged a note, supposedly written by Johnson, promising to repay a sum of money that matched the value of the tobacco Scarburgh had delivered. Once again, Anthony Johnson took a case to court. This time, however, he lost. Despite the fact that Johnson could neither read nor write, local authorities accepted the note as legal and ruled that Scarburgh could keep his tobacco.

Johnson may have continued to pursue the case, because the final distribution of his land was not made until after his death in 1670. Eventually, a Virginia jury ruled that his original land in that colony could be seized by the colony "because he was a Negroe and by consequence an alien." The 200 acres he had sold were awarded to Edmund Scarburgh. The 50 acres he had deeded to his son Richard were granted to another planter, even though Richard and his family had been living on and working the land.

Johnson's widow Mary lived on at Tonies Vineyard until her own death in 1680. Their sons managed to hold onto that property. Records of the family cease after the death of Johnson's grandson, John Jr. The legal situation for blacks in the region was becoming more and more tenuous, however. Major slave codes enacted by Virginia in 1682 became models of repression in the South for the next 180 years. Not only were blacks denied the opportunity to own land, they were also barred from meeting in large numbers, from carrying arms, and from attacking "any Christian." The era of chattel slavery had begun.

CRISPUS
ATTUCKS

(1723?–1770)

Crispus Attucks, born a slave, was the first American to die in the cause of American independence. He was killed by British soldiers in Boston, Massachusetts, in 1770, after the soldiers opened fire on a crowd of citizens protesting British occupation of their city. Prior to that event, he had lived his life in obscurity. In death, he became famous.

Little is known about Attucks's early life. According to legend, he was born in the colony of Massachusetts. His father was a black man and his mother an Indian. Both may well have been slaves, because at that time Indians were enslaved, too. Attucks was said to be an expert trader of horses and cattle and was accustomed to dealing with free white men. The story goes that he wanted to buy his freedom but that his owner, John Brown of Framingham, refused.

In the fall of 1750, Crispus Attucks ran away. His owner placed an ad in the Boston Gazette, offering a reward of ten pounds for his return. This advertisement describes Attucks's appearance, the only record of his age and the way he looked: "a Molatto Fellow, about 27

THE SPIRIT OF INDEPENDENCE

C rispus Attucks's mother may have been a descendant of John Attucks, a Natick Indian who lived in the 1660s. John Attucks was friendly with the British colonizers of Massachusetts and converted to Christianity. But during an Indian uprising that came to be known as King Philip's War, he sided with his own people. Captured by New England colonists, John Attucks was tried and executed for treason in 1676, one hundred years before the Revolutionary War.

Years of Age, named *Crispas*, 6 Feet two Inches high, short curl'd Hair, his Knees nearer together than common." The last bit of information means that he was knock-kneed.

All efforts by John Brown to get his slave back failed. Crispus managed to remain free for the next twenty years. No one knows where he went or what he did, but probably he spent those years as a sailor, working on cargo ships that sailed to the West Indies and on whaling ships off the New England coast.

During those years, the British colonists in North America chafed under the restrictions of their far-away rulers. By the late 1760s, many residents of Boston, capital of the Massachusetts colony, had become outspoken in their complaints of unfair taxation policies and the lack of free trade allowed the colonies. So restive was the city that in 1768 British King George III ordered two regiments of soldiers from British posts in Canada to sail south to Boston to maintain order. The first troops ever sent to the colonies in peacetime, they took over the Customs House and set up tents on Boston Common.

Over the next months, scattered incidents between the soldiers and the citizens led to heightened tensions. A major clash was inevitable. It came on the night of March 5, 1770, when several fights broke out. The situation got out of hand when a British private hit a barber's apprentice and the boy ran through the streets shouting that he had been "killed." Someone set the fire bells ringing.

Crispus Attucks happened to be in Boston that evening. According to a Boston slave named Andrew who knew Attucks, he had been living in New Providence, in the British colony of the Bahamas, and was in Boston en route to North Carolina. He was enjoying supper at a local inn when the fire bells started to ring. He left his meal to investigate.

A large crowd had gathered at Dock Square. Attucks picked up a large stick and shouted to the people to follow him to the Customs House. There, the soldier who had attacked the barber's apprentice was on duty. Some in the crowd began to taunt the soldier, who became frightened and called for reinforcements. One Captain Preston, in charge of the guardhouse that evening, led seven other soldiers out to help. They used their bayonets as clubs to cut through the crowd and drive it back. But the Bostonians refused to retreat. The soldiers loaded their muskets. Men in the crowd cried, "Damn them, they dare not fire, we are not afraid of them."

Crispus Attucks was standing close to the soldiers. According to the slave named Andrew, he raised his stick and struck at Captain Preston. A group of men followed him, yelling, "Kill the dogs, knock them over." The soldiers fired their muskets. Attucks took two musket balls in the chest and fell to the ground. Four other men died as well.

Three days later, thousands of the city's residents and people from the countryside attended a public funeral for the five victims. All the bells in the city tolled in their honor, and they were buried together in one grave at the city cemetery.

The soldiers involved in what later came to be called the Boston Massacre were tried for murder. John Adams was one of the lawyers who represented the soldiers. He claimed that Attucks's "mad behavior" was to blame for the event. Two soldiers were found guilty and had their hands branded as punishment.

More clashes between British soldiers and colonists occurred. King George III continued to levy unfair taxes. Within three years, Adams had changed his mind. In July 1773, he wrote in his diary a letter to Governor Thomas Hutchinson of Massachusetts. He may have intended to publish it and he signed the letter "Crispus Attucks." The letter said, in part: "You will hear from Us with Astonishment. You ought to hear from Us with Horror. You are chargeable before God and Man, with our Blood. The Soldiers were but passive Instruments. . . You was a free Agent. You acted, coolly, deliberately, with all that premeditated Malice, not against Us in Particular but against the People in general. . . . You will hear from Us hereafter."

Two years after that, the battles of Lexington and Concord, Massachusetts, touched off the War of Independence. Black minutemen were among the colonists who confronted the British soldiers from Boston that day in April 1775. Many patriots, black and white, would die in the cause of independence. But the distinction of being the first remained that of Crispus Attucks. In 1888, the black citizens of Boston succeeded in having a monument to Attucks erected on Boston Common, the earliest American public monument to a black man.

BENJAMIN
BANNEKER
(1750–1816)

Americans who favored slavery often justified their views by arguing that black people were no more capable of learning than were animals.

Then along came a man who challenged those assumptions "with the fire of his intellect," one nineteenth-century historian declared, forcing some Americans to question their belief in black inferiority.[1]

The man's name was Benjamin Banneker, and there is probably no better example of the desire to learn and to teach others than that shown by him throughout his life.

Banneker was not a teacher in the usual sense, with a classroom full of students. Instead, he taught mathematics, astronomy, history, and other subjects by publishing his knowledge in pamphlets that came out once a year.

Born to free black parents, Mary and Robert Banneker, on a farm near the Patapsco River in Baltimore County, Maryland, Benjamin Banneker had deep roots on two continents and a keen understanding of the meaning of freedom.

Benjamin had an English grandmother, Molly Welsh. In about 1683 she had been found guilty of stealing milk from a farmer. In fact, she had accidentally knocked over a pail of milk, but the mistake was costly. Molly was shipped to the American colonies as an indentured servant to pay for her crime.

After toiling for seven years on a tobacco plantation in Maryland, Molly had earned her freedom. She then bought a small farm and two slaves. One of the slaves was a man named Bannka or Banneka, who said he was the son of an African chieftain.

Within three years, Molly freed Bannka. In spite of strict laws against interracial marriages, Molly and Bannka married and had a daughter, Mary Banneky ("daughter of Bannka or Banneka"). The name was later changed to Banneker.

When Mary fell in love with a slave named Robert, her parents bought his freedom so the young couple could marry. Having no surname, Robert took his wife's family name as his own. Benjamin was the first of the four children they would have.

Benjamin's first teacher was his grandmother, Molly. She taught him to read and write by using a Bible she had imported from England. Benjamin's mind was sharp, and he soon learned all that Molly had to teach, so she sent him to a one-room school near her farm.

As he grew older, Benjamin had to work full time on his father's farm, but he continued to educate himself for the rest of his life. Few books were available at the time (Benjamin could not afford a book of his own until he was thirty-two years old), but he managed to borrow books and teach himself literature, history, and mathematics. He was so good at mathematics that visitors came from far away with practical problems or brain-teasing puzzles for him to solve.

At age twenty-two, Banneker built a striking clock without ever having seen one. First, he studied the workings of a small watch, then used a pocket knife to carve each part of his clock from wood he had collected and carefully seasoned. He used metal parts only where they

DIVING INTO BOOKS

Benjamin Banneker went to a school that accepted both black and white students. It was open only during the winter months, when the children did not have to work on their parents' farms. The few years Benjamin spent there constituted the only formal education he ever received. Jacob Hall, one of Banneker's black classmates, said Benjamin showed little interest in fun and games. Instead, Hall recalled, "all his delight was to dive into his books."[2]

were absolutely needed. It was the first clock of its kind in the Maryland region.

Banneker enjoyed the mathematical challenge of calculating the proper ratio of the many gears, wheels, and other parts, then fitting them together to move in harmony. His clock operated for more than forty years, striking the hours of six and twelve. Visitors came from miles around to see the amazing achievement of this self-taught man.

One day, a friendly Quaker neighbor named George Ellicott lent Banneker a telescope, some other instruments, and several books on astronomy. From that moment on, the study of astronomy dominated Banneker's life. He often spent entire nights studying the stars, after working all day on the farm. Eventually, the Ellicott family bought part of Banneker's farm. They agreed to pay him enough money each year to live on, and thus enabled him to spend the last sixteen years of his life studying astronomy full time.

Banneker's studies progressed rapidly, and he began making all the calculations necessary for an almanac for the Delaware, Maryland, Pennsylvania, and Virginia regions. But his work was suddenly interrupted by a request from his neighbor, George Ellicott, to help survey a 10-square-mile area known as the Federal Territory (now Washington, D.C.). Congress had decided to build a new national capital there, and one of George Ellicott's cousins, Major Andrew Ellicott, was appointed by President George Washington to head the survey.

So it was that Banneker, at age sixty, was hired by Secretary of State Thomas Jefferson and spent several months in 1791 helping to lay out the capital. Thomas Jefferson had earlier claimed that black people lacked intellectual skills, and the arrival of Banneker as a member of the surveying team led to the following comment in the *Georgetown Weekly Ledger:*

"Some time last month arrived in this town Mr. Andrew Ellicott [*sic*] . . . He is attended by Benjamin Banniker [*sic*], an Ethiopian, whose abilities, as a surveyor, and an astronomer, clearly prove that Mr. Jefferson's concluding that race of men were void of mental endowments, was without foundation."[3]

Banneker spent several months making and recording astronomical observations, maintaining the field astronomical clock, and compiling other data required by Ellicott. This work made him more interested than ever in astronomy, and when he returned home, he spent countless nighttime hours at his telescope. On many nights, instead of using the telescope, the old man wrapped himself in a blanket and lay in a field watching the stars until dawn.

During the day, he worked at astronomical calculations for each day of the coming year (1792), and completed them in just a few weeks. At last he was ready to publish his precious almanac.

With the help of the anti-slavery societies, the almanac—*Benjamin Banneker's Pennsylvania, Delaware, Maryland and Virginia Almanack and Ephemeris, for the Year of Our Lord, 1792; Being Bissextile, or Leap-Year, and the Sixteenth Year of American Independence, which commenced July 4, 1776* was published in Baltimore and was a huge success.

Many colonists owned Bibles, but an almanac was usually the only other book in their homes. An almanac contained a calendar with astronomical information about each day, such as the rising and setting of the sun and the moon, phases of the moon, positions of the planets, and other observations about nature. This information was especially prized at a time when most Americans made their living from farming. They used the observations to try to determine the best time to plant and harvest their crops.

The first almanac sold in great numbers, and Banneker published one every year for the next four years. The almanacs brought him international fame. He used that fame to prove that African Americans were as capable as anyone of learning and teaching.

He sent a copy of his almanac to Thomas Jefferson, one of the framers of the Declaration of Independence and U.S. Constitution, along with a letter denouncing slavery and pointing out "that one universal Father hath . . . endued [sic] us all with the same faculties . . ."[4]

Jefferson, a slave owner himself, was apparently moved by Banneker's arguments against slavery and impressed by the almanac. He sent a copy of it to his friend the Marquis de Condorcet, secretary of the Academy of Sciences in Paris. Jefferson wrote, "I am happy to inform you that we have now in the United States a negro . . . who is a very respectable mathematician."[5]

Rarely leaving the farm where he was born, Benjamin Banneker used the power of his mind to discover things and give useful, accurate information to others throughout the almost seventy-five years of his life. Banneker continued to make his beloved calculations until a few months before his death on October 9, 1806.

Benjamin Banneker's almanacs contained important information on the movements of the sun, moon, stars, and planets, and helped many farmers determine the best time to plant.

MARIE-THÉRÈSE
METOYER

(1742–1816)

Blacks were entrepreneurs in America from early colonial times. Years before the Declaration of Independence, one of the most successful of all was born. Marie-Thérèse Metoyer took her first breath in Natchitoches, Louisiana, when Louisiana was still a French colony. Known as Coincoin, a name given to second-born daughters by the Ewe people of western Africa, she probably had at least one parent who was an Ewe. Her parents, François and Françoise, were slaves and had been married in Natchitoches. In the French colonies, slave marriages were legal.

Coincoin's family was owned by Louis Juchereau de Saint-Denis, a commandant in the French army and founder of the army post where they lived. When he died, his ownership of Coincoin passed on to his widow and then to his son, who gave her to his daughter, Marie. During those years, Coincoin gave birth to five children, each one baptized in the Catholic Church. All were sold away from her, but she never forgot them.

Marie de Saint-Denis rented Coincoin to Claude-Thomas-Pierre Metoyer, a French merchant on Isle Brevelle in the Red River valley of Louisiana. Watching Coincoin toil as a servant in his household, Metoyer fell in love with her, and together they had four children. Eventually Metoyer purchased and freed her, along with their new-born child. She remained with him another eight years, bearing three more children—all legally free because she was now free, too.

In 1786, Claude-Thomas-Pierre Metoyer married someone else. But first he arranged for Coincoin to receive a small plot of land and an annual sum to support herself and her children who were free. At the age of forty-four, Coincoin began a new life. One of the first things she did was to purchase her eldest daughter, Marie-Louise. She had been crippled in a shooting accident and cost only $300. Coincoin's plan was to buy back all of her other enslaved children, but first she had to make more money.

Coincoin planted tobacco and indigo and raised cattle and turkeys, all of which she sold. She also trapped bear and sold their hides and grease.

FREEDOM FOR . . . WHOM?

While building her ranch, Coincoin became a slaveowner herself. Freed blacks were often permitted to purchase slaves who were not family members, but they were not always allowed to set them free.

By the time of Coincoin's death in 1816 at the age of seventy-four, she owned sixteen slaves. Coincoin's descendants inherited her energy, spirit, and talent for business. Before the Civil War, they built an agricultural empire on Isle Brevelle that included nearly 20,000 acres of land, a dozen homes, and, ironically, 500 slaves.

In the course of 400 years, more than 15 million Africans were captured and shipped to the New World. Those who survived the passage—and their children from generation to generation—were sold like cattle to the highest bidders. (Library of Congress)

In 1762, France ceded a large part of Louisiana Province to Spain, including all territory west of the Mississippi River. By 1794, Coincoin had established herself financially and secured land from the Spanish government. She obtained a grant of 640 acres of piney woods on Isle Brevelle. There she herded cattle and raised crops, profiting handsomely from her hard work and smart business practices.

Now she could purchase more of her children. They were scattered throughout western Louisiana and eastern Texas. She would have to travel to find them and negotiate their sale. Nearly all their owners were willing to sell them, for cash or on credit. Sadly, she was unable to purchase one daughter, Françoise, but she and her heirs managed to buy Françoise's children.

In 1802, at the age of sixty, Coincoin offered to forfeit the annual payment Metoyer gave her in exchange for the freedom of their first three children. Metoyer agreed, and Coincoin at last realized her dream of freedom for her almost entire family.

Coincoin's home on Isle Brevelle, Melrose Plantation, still stands. It has been designated a National Historic Landmark.

JEAN BAPTISTE
POINT DU SABLE

(1745?–1818)

Another colonial entrepreneur of French heritage was Jean Baptiste Point du Sable. He was born in the town of St. Marc in Santo Domingo in the West Indies around 1745, of mixed French and African parentage. His French father was a sea captain. His mother, whose name was Suzanne, was a slave. She died when du Sable was ten.

When he was an adolescent, du Sable was sent to school in France, which was customary among the well-to-do French in the West Indies. He attended a school outside Paris and met a fellow there from Martinigue named Jacques Clemorgan, with whom he became close friends.

Returning to Santo Domingo after completing his schooling, du Sable worked for some years on his father's ships. But he was an adventurous young man and yearned to see more of the world. He was especially interested in visiting the southern part of North

America, where France had established the colony of Louisiana. His father understood and encouraged him to pursue his dreams. Presented with a ship named *Suzanne* by his father, du Sable and his friend Jacques Clemorgan set out for North America.

They had reached the Gulf of Mexico when they were struck by a hurricane. The raging winds and towering waves smashed the *Suzanne* to pieces. Both du Sable and Clemorgan were injured and were lucky to be rescued by a passing boat and taken to the port of New Orleans.

Another kind of danger awaited them there. New Orleans was a French port, but it was under the control of the Spanish. It was also a major slave-trading port. Du Sable and his friend had lost their identity papers to the hurricane, and without papers they were in danger of being enslaved. The French Jesuits, a Catholic order, protected du Sable and Clemorgan until they were well enough to travel again. After a time with the Jesuit priests, the friends decided to travel farther north, following the Mississippi River and trapping for furs and trading with the Indians along the way. They made their way upriver to French-held territory in the North American midwest. Leaving the Mississippi at St. Louis, they began trading with local Indians and soon had a thriving business. But political turmoil intervened.

Between 1689 and 1763, a series of wars had raged between the French and British for control of territories in North America. Called the French and Indian Wars by the British, they pitted England against France and its Indian allies in North America and were campaigns in a worldwide struggle for empire between the two nations. With the Treaty of Paris in 1763, France ceded control of Canada to Great Britain. In the years that followed, the British also took over French-held territories to the South. In 1767, St. Louis came under British control. Being of French heritage and French-speaking, du Sable and Clemorgan left St. Louis.

They continued on to the Illinois territory, where they settled among the Peoria and Potowatomi Indians. Du Sable met and married a Potowatomi girl named Kittihawa, who was also known as Catherine, in an Indian marriage ceremony. He was inducted into his wife's clan. The couple's first son, named Jean Baptiste after his father, was born near Fort Peoria in Illinois territory. But du Sable had not gotten over his wanderlust, and he set off again to explore the North American wilderness. Whether or not his friend Jacques Clemorgan went with him is not known; he may have remained in Peoria.

Du Sable traveled north toward Canada, following the Illinois River, trapping and trading along the way. At the main portage point between the river and Lake Michigan, he found a low swampy area that the local Indians called Eschikagou, which means "place of bad smells." It was bug-ridden and unpleasant, but du Sable realized it was also a key transfer station for anyone traveling northward. He determined to set up a trading post there.

Du Sable returned to Fort Peoria and persuaded his wife's clan to accompany him back to Eschikagou. On his return, he built a house for his family that also served as a trading post. The other members of the clan built houses of their own, and soon they had created a small settlement. As du Sable had anticipated, he was soon doing a good business, and as he prospered he added a bake house, a dairy, a poultry house, a smoke house for curing meats, a stable, a workshop, and a mill powered by horses. He and Catherine had a second child, a daughter named Suzanne. The settlement expanded, and du Sable's trading post acquired a reputation as the best one between St. Louis and Montreal.

While du Sable was establishing himself and his new settlement, the Revolutionary War began in 1776. France sided with the British colonists seeking their independence from England, and du Sable's French heritage put him under suspicion. It was assumed because of his French-speaking background that he was sympathetic to the

French, and in 1779 the English commander of the area that included Chicago had du Sable arrested as a spy.

Du Sable was taken to the prison at Fort Mackinac in what is now Michigan. Although technically a prisoner, he was well treated and even allowed to hunt and fish in the area surrounding the fort. After a year, his British captors decided he was not a threat and freed him. Du Sable returned to Chicago, where he resumed his life with his family. Ten years later, and twenty-four years after their Indian wedding ceremony, he and Catherine were married by a Catholic priest at Cahokia, Illinois. His businesses continued to prosper, and he increased his holdings and his wealth. Chicago was established as a city and continued to thrive. Du Sable's daughter, Suzanne, married a man named Michael Derais. Their daughter, Eulalie, born in 1796, is considered the first child born in the city of Chicago.

In 1800, when he was in his fifties, du Sable decided it was time to retire. He sold all his holdings in Chicago to a man named John Lalime for twelve hundred dollars, a substantial sum in those days. A local man named John Kinzie served as legal witness to the sale and then carried the bill of sale to be legally filed in St. Joseph, Missouri. This act led to later confusion over who had owned the trading post and who could be credited with the founding of Chicago.

Du Sable and his family moved back to Peoria. His longtime friend Jacques Clemorgan had remained there. After Catherine's death there in 1809, du Sable relocated to St. Charles, Missouri, where his daughter and her family lived. Du Sable died in St. Charles on August 28, 1818, and was buried in St. Borromeo Cemetery there.

At some point, a plaque had been installed in Chicago crediting the founding of the settlement to du Sable. But the plaque was removed in 1927. John Kinzie, who had carried the bill of sale for du Sable's Chicago property to St. Joseph, Missouri, was instead credited as the city's founder. In 1961, a museum of African American history was established in Chicago and named for du Sable. In 1968, the State of Illinois and the city of Chicago officially recognized him as the "Father of Chicago." A marker was placed on his grave that restored the credit to the man to whom it belonged. His importance in American history has also been commemorated by the U.S. Postal Service, which issued a stamp in his honor.

PRIVATE PETER

SALEM

(1750–1816)

Like du Sable, Peter Salem was later honored on a commemorative stamp. Salem was one of the 5,000 African Americans who served in the Revolutionary War. Also called Salem Middleux, he was born a slave in Framingham, Massachusetts. He belonged, according to some sources, to Captain Jeremiah Belknap, who later sold him to a Major Lawson of Buckminster, Massachusetts, a town near Boston.

In 1775, the American colonists' Continental army prepared to face the British occupying troops. The people of Boston readied for battle, and so did Peter Salem. He enlisted in the First Massachusetts Regiment as a private in Captain Simon Edgel's company and was granted his freedom.

Salem was at the April 1775 Battle of Lexington, against British Major John Pitcairn. He was also at Concord. Those battles marked the beginning of the Revolutionary War. On June 17, 1775, the colonists and British redcoats squared off at Bunker Hill. More than twenty-five blacks were in the colonial ranks. Private Peter Salem was among

36

them—as a servant to Lieutenant Grosvenor, who was facing Major Pitcairn a second time.

As the British advanced, colonial officers rode back and forth among the troops. "Don't fire 'til you see the whites of their eyes!" they urged. Peter Salem obeyed orders as long as he could. The king's soldiers charged. In the lead, Major Pitcairn called out, "The day is ours!" Then a bullet from Private Peter Salem's gun shot him through. The colonists eventually drove the British from the hill and showed their enemy that they were a force to be reckoned with.

Although some observers said that several bullets brought Major Pitcairn down, most regarded Peter Salem as the hero. According to one report, they took up a collection to send Salem to General George Washington as the man who had slain Pitcairn.

The artist John Trumbull witnessed the battle from Roxbury, across the harbor from Bunker Hill, and possibly met Salem within the next few days. Trumbull painted the climactic scene ten years later, in London. He worked from memory and probably used a black model in his studio to represent Peter Salem. In the lower right section of the painting, Salem stands close behind Lieutenant Grosvenor, holding a French Charleville musket of the sort that fired the fatal bullet into Pitcairn.

Salem stayed with the Continental army, participating in the critical Battle of Saratoga in 1777, among others. With the American victory over the British in 1783, Salem left the army. That same year he married Katie Benson and settled in Leicester, Massachusetts, as a basket weaver. Eventually, he returned to Framingham, where he died in the town's poorhouse on August 16, 1816.

For some years after the Revolutionary War, engravings based on John Trumbull's painting included Peter Salem in a prominent position. But by 1855, according to William C. Nell, a black historian of the time, Salem was less visible: "In more recent editions, his figure is *non est inventus*. A significant but inglorious omission."[1]

REVOLTS AND REBELLIONS

Long before the first shots at Lexington and Concord, there were huge rebellions against colonial rulers in the New World. In 1729, escaped slaves in Jamaica called Maroons were already waging a war against the British government. In 1739, they won their freedom and some of the British-held land. In 1751, 3,000 Maroons in the Caribbean island of St. Domingue (modern Haiti and the Dominican Republic) revolted against the island's French colonial government. They lost their struggle at that time, but eventually won their freedom in 1800, led by revolutionary hero Toussaint L'Ouverture (1743–1803), the first ruler of independent Haiti.

In 1882, the citizens of Framingham built a monument to the memory of Peter Salem. For many years, the Freedman's Bank of Boston printed his picture on their banknotes. The Daughters of the American Revolution bought Salem's home in 1909 and turned it into a historic site. In 1968, the federal government made a commemorative stamp of the Trumbull painting that included Peter Salem.

PRIVATE AUSTIN
DABNEY

(?–?)

Peter Salem had voluntarily enlisted in the Continental army, but Austin Dabney was sent in his master's stead. Born a slave in North Carolina, the son of a slave woman and her master, Dabney was owned by a Georgia colonist named Aycock. At the time, a colonist who did not wish to serve in the army could send a slave or servant in his place. Aycock sent Austin Dabney.

Dabney served as an artilleryman in the Battle of Battle Creek, Georgia. On February 4, 1779, a musket ball ripped through his thigh. Left on the battleground, he was found by a white soldier named Harris, who took him home and cared for him until he recovered. According to legend, Dabney never forgot Harris's kindness and served the family faithfully for years afterward. Much later, the Harris family's eldest son found a way to thank Dabney for his loyalty and self-sacrifice.

When the Harris family moved to Madison County, Georgia, Dabney went with them. His hard work and saving made it possible for the eldest Harris son to go to Franklin College. When young Harris

got a job in the office of state legislator Stephen Upson, he sought Upson's help for Dabney. Upson persuaded the Georgia Assembly to award Dabney a pension for his service in the Revolutionary War.

In 1819, the government held a lottery for land. It was only for Revolutionary War veterans. Although a pensioner, Dabney was not allowed in the lottery because he was black. After protests from Harris and others, the Georgia Assembly cited Dabney's "bravery and fortitude" in "several engagements and actions," and passed an act awarding Dabney 112 acres of land in Walton County, Georgia.[1] But a group of whites in Madison County protested the award, claiming "it was an indignity to white men, for a mulatto to be put upon an equality with them in the distribution of the public lands."[2]

To collect his pension, Dabney traveled once a year to Savannah. On one occasion he encountered the governor of Georgia, who recognized him and invited him into his home as an honored guest. Dabney prospered. He owned fine horses and attended races and bet on horses. But when the young Harris moved away from Madison County, Dabney went with him. Dabney died in Zebulon, Georgia.

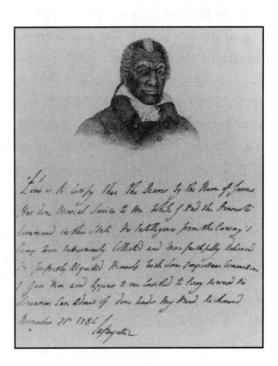

Another African American patriot, James Armistead, became an undercover agent for the Continental army. For his service, he received this commendation from the Marquis de Lafayette.

PHILLIS
WHEATLEY

(1753?–1784)

In the summer of 1761, a ship named the *Phillis* arrived in Boston. A small and fragile girl, no more than eight years old, stood shivering at the dock. Sickness and fear consumed her trembling body, which she attempted to cover with an old piece of carpet.

Kidnapped from Africa and sold into slavery, Phillis was named for the slave ship on which she was brought to America. Her birthplace is unknown, but research has placed the point of her capture on the west coast of Africa, the present-day nations of Senegal and Gambia. How frightening it must have been for Phillis—first, to be torn away from her family and village, and then to endure the cruel voyage.

This young girl was destined to become one of colonial America's brightest stars. A future poet and author of the first collection of poetry by an African American, she was at that moment a piece of property awaiting the highest bidder. Along with approximately 75 other Africans, she was part of the human cargo of Captain Peter Gwinn, who worked for Timothy Fitch, slave merchant and owner of the *Phillis*.

PHILLIS WHEATLEY NEGRO SERVANT to Mr. JOHN WHEATLEY, of BOSTON.

Along with the small number of survivors, young Phillis had been splashed with a bucket of water and was presented for sale at the Boston docks. Among the speculators at the Boston slave auction was Susannah Wheatley, wife of John Wheatley, a wealthy Boston tailor. The mother of 18-year-old twins, Mary and Nathaniel Wheatley, Susannah was in search of a young servant of "healthy" appearance. Something about the trembling and half-naked girl captured her attention. Perhaps it was Susannah's own poor health, or that of her fragile daughter, Mary, that evoked such pity and made her choose the sickly girl.

Phillis Wheatley's tribal and religious African roots are not known. But based on her point of capture and on her own early recollections, some historians believe that she was a member of the Fulani, a Muslim tribe of western Africa. As a girl, she shared a story of a faint memory of her mother kneeling before the sunrise, a Muslim ritual.

Whatever religious grounding young Phillis may have had, it was displaced by the influence of Christianity, the religion of her owners, whose customs she accepted.

Phillis quickly adjusted to life in the Wheatley household, where she would remain for 17 years. The Wheatleys recognized the young

AFRICANS IN COLONIAL TIMES

When Phillis arrived in America, 230,000 blacks lived in the colonies. Some 16,000, like Phillis, were enslaved in New England, where they worked primarily as servants and were allowed to learn to read and write. But most were enslaved in the South, where they labored on rice, cotton, and tobacco plantations. Southern "slave codes" denied blacks many privileges: learning to read or write, defending themselves against abuse by whites, testifying against whites in court, and owning property.

slave girl's hunger for knowledge and encouraged her. Eighteen-year-old Mary Wheatley, who was sickly like Phillis, became a constant companion. The two spent extended periods of time reading the Bible and studying poetry. Phillis Wheatley soon learned to read English, and by age nine was studying Latin and the Bible.

At age 12, she began to write poetry. The Wheatleys provided paper, pen, and ink and allowed her to burn a candle until late into the night. Because of her poor health, Phillis was virtually cut off from other African Americans, so she found companionship in words. The Wheatleys treated Phillis differently from their other slaves. They assigned her light household duties, such as the dusting and polishing of furniture or the arranging of tables for dinner parties. They even scolded Prince, their driver, for keeping Phillis up front beside him in the cold, damp weather, instead of letting her sit inside their carriage.

The one close relationship that Phillis was able to develop with another slave was with Obour Tanner. They met in Rhode Island, where their owners were on vacation. Like Phillis, Tanner was educated by her owners and was a devout Christian. The two young women established a long friendship through their letters.

Phillis Wheatley started to gain recognition in 1770 with the publication of a verse she wrote in 1767 in memory of the Reverend George Whitefield, a famed Methodist evangelist. In 1768, she wrote a patriotic verse, "On the Arrival of the Ships of War, and Landing of the Troops," in response to the arrival in Boston of British troops sent to quell colonial unrest.

Phillis became a source of great pride to the Wheatley family, and they began to invite prominent Bostonians to meet and hear her. Among those invited was Eunice Fitch, wife of the merchant upon whose slave ship Phillis had arrived in America. Governor Thomas Hutchins and legislator John Hancock gave the aspiring young artist books to encourage her.

In 1773, Nathaniel Wheatley had cause to travel to England on business. The family decided that Phillis Wheatley would accompany him on the trip. They had a special reason. American printers had refused to publish the writings of a slave girl, so Nathaniel Wheatley took Phillis to London to publish her book. She gave it the title *Poems on Various Subjects, Religious and Moral, by Phillis Wheatley, Negro Servant to Mrs. Wheatley of Boston.*

Her visit to London was glorious. To Phillis's surprise, word of her accomplishment as a poet had reached England before her arrival. London society embraced her. She became a protégée of both Lady Huntingdon and Lord Darmouth, who was then mayor of London. Other dignitaries who welcomed and encouraged her included Benjamin Franklin, who later became a prominent political figure in America, and Brooke Watson, who would become the mayor of London.

Unfortunately, Susannah Wheatley became severely ill, and Phillis's stay in London had to end. She left London a few weeks short of the publication of her book. She was approximately 20 years old when she returned to Boston in September 1773. It would prove an eventful month for Phillis Wheatley. She was emancipated by John Wheatley and her book was released.

Some individuals who believed that people of African heritage were incapable of "thinking," let alone "writing," questioned that Phillis was the genuine author of the book. So her mistress, Susannah Wheatley, decided to prove that Phillis was indeed the true author. Thus, a certificate signed by prominent white men of New England was printed in the book. It read in part: "We whose names are under-written, do assure the world that the poems specified in the following pages were (as verily we believe) written by Phillis, a young Negro girl." Susannah Wheatley died shortly afterward.

Phillis Wheatley continued to write poetry right up to the beginning of the American Revolution. She wrote to and was acknowledged by General George Washington in 1775. The general invited her to visit his headquarters, which she did the following year. Altogether, Phillis would publish five books of poetry and letters.

Following the death of John Wheatley in 1778, Phillis, who had remained part of the Wheatley household, was now on her own. That same year she married John Peters. Stories about her husband vary. Some say that John Peters held a variety of jobs—lawyer, grocer, banker, and doctor— but that he was unsuccessful in all of these occupations. Others label him a ne'er-do-well who shunned hard labor. It is difficult, however, to determine Peters's true character given the prejudice of the day. Whatever the true story, serious financial problems landed him in debtor's jail in 1784.

Phillis gave birth to three children, two of whom died as infants. Her third child died in 1784. Phillis died soon after on December 7, 1784, destitute and living in a boardinghouse in Boston. Announcement of her funeral appeared in two local papers: "Last Lord's Day, died Mrs. Phillis Peters (formerly Phillis Wheatley) aged 31, known to the world by her celebrated miscellaneous poems. Her funeral is to be this afternoon at four o'clock. . . . Her friends and acquaintances are desired to attend." Sadly, no one came.

Although Phillis Wheatley's five books were ignored for years after her death, and often dismissed as being too sentimental and

A POET SHARES HER FEELINGS

"In every human breast, God has implanted a principle, which we call love of freedom; it is impatient of oppression and pants for deliverance. I will assert that same principle lives in us."

—Phillis Wheatley

patriotic, today her work is given the special honor it deserves. Indeed, a debt of gratitude is owed this early American poet for her discipline and determination. With the site of her grave unknown, the city of Boston honored her some 200 years after her death by erecting a monument in her name.

PRIVATE LEMUEL
HAYNES

(1753–1833)

Born around the same time as Phillis Wheatley, Lemuel Haynes was another African American man who fought in the Revolutionary War. His mother was a white woman, and his father was a black man whom he never knew. Shortly after his birth on July 18, 1753, in West Hartford, Connecticut, Haynes was given up as a baby. On just one occasion later, Haynes met his mother by accident. She pretended not to know him, and he furiously reproached her. Even as a child, he had a strong sense of right and wrong.

"When I was five months old, I was carried to Granville, Massachusetts, to be a servant to Deacon David Rose till I was Twenty-one. He was a man of singular piety. I was taught the principles of religion,"[1] recalled Lemuel Haynes about his life before the Revolutionary War. The Roses were farmers, and young Lemuel helped them clear land and plant crops. There was little time left over for school. When he did go, he attended a common school with white children. He loved reading and spent his evenings poring over the Bible and

books of psalms by the light of the fire. As he grew older, he read to the Rose family in the evenings.

One night, he slipped a sermon he had written into the book and read it to the family. Deacon David Rose was impressed. Since the parish had no minister, Rose asked his young servant to conduct the service and read an approved sermon, sometimes written by Lemuel.

By 1774, war clouds were gathering on the horizon of the British colonies in North America. Haynes stood up for his belief in freedom and joined the Minute Men, the colonial militia established by the Massachusetts provincial congress. Every week, he and his comrades practiced for battle in case they were needed. Soon enough, they were. After the Battle of Lexington, Massachusetts, in April 1775, Haynes accompanied Captain Lebbeus Ball's militia company to join the Continental army at Roxbury, Massachusetts. In 1776, Haynes marched in the expedition to Fort Ticonderoga, where with Ethan Allen and the Green Mountain Boys he helped to take the fort from British General Burgoyne's army.

Forty years later, in a sermon delivered on George Washington's birthday, Haynes would remind his listeners of his service in the Revolution: "Perhaps it is not ostentatious in the speaker to observe, that in early life he devoted all for the sake of freedom and independence, and endured frequent campaigns in their defence. . . ."[2]

Returning home from the war, Haynes put down his gun and took up the Bible again. In 1779, a clergyman in New Canaan, Connecticut, helped him learn Latin. Another supporter got him a teaching job and tutored him in Greek. Now Haynes could read the New Testament as originally written.

On November 29, 1780, after taking an examination in languages, sciences, and the gospel, Haynes became a preacher. A Congregational church in Middle Granville invited him to be its pastor, and he served that church for several years.

While in Granville, Haynes married Elizabeth Babbitt, a white former schoolteacher. They had ten children—seven girls and three boys.

In 1785, Haynes was officially ordained a minister of the gospel by an association of ministers in Litchfield, Connecticut. That same year, he accepted a position as pastor at a church in Torrington, Connecticut, becoming the first black pastor of a white church in the United States. One parishioner deliberately kept his hat on in church as a sign of disrespect. When the self-confident Reverend Haynes approached the pulpit, he either did not see or did not pay attention to the slight but began preaching. According to Haynes's biographer, Timothy Cooley, the parishioner later recalled, "My hat was instantly taken off and thrown under the seat, and I found myself listening with the most profound attention."[3]

But others did not come around, and the snubs of a determined clique in the congregation forced Haynes to leave Torrington after two years.

In March 1788, Haynes accepted a pastorship with a church in Rutland, Vermont, where he remained for thirty years. He was active in political and church circles throughout New England, speaking out on the moral wrong of slavery.

"I am pointing you to the poor Africans among us," he wrote in 1801. "What has reduced them to their present pitiful, abject state? Is it any distinction that the god of nature hath made in their formation? Nay—but being subjected to slavery, by the cruel hands of oppressors, they have been taught to view themselves as a rank of beings far below others, which has suppressed in a degree, every principle of manhood, and so they become despised, ignorant, and licentious. This should fill us with the utmost detestation against every attack on the rights of men. . . ."[4]

In 1804, Haynes was presented with a master of arts degree from Middlebury College in Vermont, thus becoming the first black person to receive an honorary degree from a white college in the United States.

Eventually, Haynes returned to Granville, Massachusetts. He spent the last eleven years of his life there and died on September 28, 1833, at the age of eighty.

PAUL
CUFFE
(1759–1817)

◆

Paul Cuffe was a ship captain who prospered following the Revolutionary War. In 1795, he sailed his 69-ton schooner *Ranger* into Norfolk, Virginia, to purchase a cargo of corn. He later wrote in his autobiography of the day the ship dropped anchor and he and his crew of blacks went ashore: "The people were filled with astonishment and alarm. A vessel owned and commanded by a black man, and manned with a crew of the same complexion, was unprecedented and surprising. The white inhabitants were struck with apprehensions of the injurious effects on the minds of their slaves, suspecting that he [Cuffe] wished secretly to kindle the spirit of rebellion, and excite a destructive revolt among them."[1]

Cuffe, one of the few black men of his time to own a ship, was angered by this kind of reaction. But he did not let the concerns of whites—in Norfolk or elsewhere—interfere with his plans. He went about his business, purchased his cargo, and set sail for Connecticut, his home.

Paul Cuffe was born on the island of Cuttyhunk, off the coast of

54

PAUL

CAPTAIN

CUFFEE

1812.

From a Drawing by JOHN POLE, M. D. of Bristol, E

New Bedford, Massachusetts. He was the seventh of ten children of Cuffe Slocum and his wife, Ruth Moses, a Wampanoag Indian. Cuffe Slocum had been born in Africa and brought to the North American colonies as a slave. But he had managed to purchase his freedom from his master in Dartmouth, Massachusetts, and his children were born free.

Cuffe Slocum died when Paul was only thirteen. Although still a boy, Paul knew he would have to provide for himself. First, he found a tutor and learned to read and write. Then he studied navigation. At the age of sixteen, he went to sea, shipping out on a whaler bound for the Gulf of Mexico.

During Cuffe's third voyage, in 1776, the Revolutionary War broke out. His ship was captured by the British, and he spent three months in a New York prison. Cuffe settled in Westport, Connecticut, after his release. Because going to sea during the war was hazardous, he worked as a hired hand on a farm. Meanwhile, he continued to study navigation and to look for ways to make a better living. He and his brother John built an open boat in which they could trade with towns on the Connecticut shore, but rough seas and pirates loyal to England made that entrepreneurial venture too dangerous. The brothers returned to laboring on a farm as the war continued.

Paul Cuffe was still determined to make a living as a merchant mariner. Twice, he built small boats and attempted to trade. His first boat was seized by American pirates who supported the British. During his second attempt, he failed to sell his cargo of goods. Finally, on his third attempt, he managed to make such a good profit that he was able to buy an 18-ton craft and hire help.

A few years after the Revolutionary War, Cuffe married Alice Pequit, who, like his mother, was a Wampanoag Indian. He rented a small house in Westport and used his new boat to sail to Ontario, Canada, where he bought a cargo of dried codfish. Back home, he sold his cargo quickly.

THE SPIRIT OF 1776

The Cuffes were keenly aware that one reason behind the revolt of the colonies against England was the charge of "no taxation without representation." If the colonists refused to pay taxes to England because they had no say in how the English government was conducted, why should the Cuffes pay taxes to the state of Connecticut? As black men, they could not legally vote, so they refused to pay taxes. In December 1780, Paul and John Cuffe were jailed for nonpayment of taxes.

Released from prison the following spring, the Cuffes pursued their cause, putting the issue before a town meeting in Taunton, Connecticut, where they had been jailed. The Cuffes, along with five other blacks, demanded that free Negroes have the same rights as whites to vote or else be relieved of taxation. The Cuffes finally had to pay the taxes they owed, but they had put up a courageous fight for the same rights for which the white colonists had gone to war.

Over the next ten years, often in partnership with one of his brothers-in-law, Michael Wainer, also a seaman, Cuffe made greater profits and built larger vessels.

He then entered the expanding whaling business, sailing on the 42-ton schooner *Mary* in 1793. He personally harpooned two whales. He then traveled to Philadelphia to exchange whale oil and bone for hardware to outfit the *Ranger*, the 69-ton schooner that he piloted to Norfolk, Virginia, on what was probably his first trip south.

Cuffe took the corn he bought in Virginia and sold it in Westport. When the market for corn was not good, he dealt in gypsum, a mineral used in the making of plaster. He traded in whatever commodity would bring him profits. Cuffe's longest voyage of trade was on the 268-ton *Alpha*. With its black crew of seven, he sailed south to Wilmington and Savannah, then across the ocean to Helsingör, Denmark, and Göteborg, Sweden, and returned to Philadelphia with passengers and freight.

By the time Captain Paul Cuffe was fifty years old, he owned a small fleet of ships. He built a schoolhouse for Westport with his own money on his own land and then donated both land and building "freely . . . to the use of the public."[2]

Every year, however, he became more and more outraged over slavery, which he described as the "evil of one brother making merchandise of and holding his brother in bondage." He eventually decided that the best course for freed slaves was to return to their native Africa. One day in the fall of 1810, he and a crew of nine black seamen set sail for Sierra Leone in western Africa. He stayed there three months, taking notes on the country's possibilities as a home for blacks from North America. He made one more visit to Sierra Leone before returning there in 1815 on the *Traveller* with thirty-eight black emigrants and a cargo of supplies to get them started in their new home. Cuffe's health soon failed, and he died in October 1817. His dreams of an African nation of black emigrants from America would be carried forth by others and bear fruit in the settling of Liberia by African American freedmen in 1821. But there would never be a large exodus of free blacks from the United States. Free people of color in Richmond, Virginia, even declared in January 1817 that they preferred to be "colonized in the most remote corner of the land of our nativity, to being exiled" in Africa.[3]

Cuffe Farm at 1504 Drift Road in Westport, Connecticut, is now a National Historic Landmark.

RICHARD
ALLEN
(1760–1831)

The years following the American Revolution saw the development of the first black institutions. The most important were black churches. Born a slave in Philadelphia, Richard Allen helped to found the first independent black denomination.

Allen's owner was a Quaker lawyer named Benjamin Chew, who would serve as chief justice of Pennsylvania during the Revolutionary War. Chew sold the Allen family—father, mother, and four children—to Stokeley Sturgis, a small slaveholder who worked a farm outside Dover, Delaware. Unlike some other owners, Sturgis allowed his slaves to attend religious services. These included services held by the local Methodist Society, even though Methodism was opposed to slavery at that time.

Allen responded to the preaching of traveling Methodist ministers and decided to join the Methodist church. An older brother of Allen's did so as well. Sturgis permitted the Allens to join the church, despite warnings from fellow slaveholders that allowing his slaves such freedom would make them unfit servants. On hearing what their owner's

A God to Glorify

Methodism is a Protestant faith established in England in 1729 by a group of students at Oxford University. Its founders, who included John Wesley, considered the Father of Methodism, preached the doctrines of Christian perfection and personal salvation through faith. Opposition from the English clergy prevented the Methodists from speaking at parish churches, so Methodists often held meetings in the open air. Wesley, in particular, sought to minister to the poor, and a strong social consciousness became a hallmark of the Methodist tradition. Methodism was brought to the United States by immigrants from both Ireland and England. In 1769, John Wesley sent his first missionaries to America. Francis Asbury, commissioned in 1771, was the missionary most instrumental in establishing the American Methodist church.

neighbors were saying, the Allens discussed the problem and together decided that they would prove them wrong. They worked especially hard, and as Allen later wrote in his autobiography, "At length, our master said he was convinced that religion made slaves better and not worse, and often boasted of his slaves for their honesty and industry."[1]

Sturgis began to pay attention to Methodist teachings himself and eventually felt guilty about owning slaves. He proposed to the Allens that they purchase their freedom, and in 1780 Allen paid Sturgis the price settled upon and became a free man.

Allen then became a traveling preacher. Supporting himself by doing odd jobs along the way, he walked as far as South Carolina and New York, preaching to all who would listen. In many cases, his audiences were primarily white. Then, in 1786, he was summoned by the Methodist elder in charge in Philadelphia. The black congregation of St. George's Methodist Episcopal Church in that city was growing rapidly, and they needed a black minister to preach separate services for blacks.

Arriving in Philadelphia, Allen was assigned to preach a service at five o'clock in the morning, a task he regarded as "a great cross to bear." At first, he intended to stay for only about two weeks. But he found so many black Philadelphians eager to hear him that soon he was preaching four and five times a day in various parts of the city and conducting prayer meetings wherever space could be found. He encouraged black membership in St. George's church and collected contributions that helped the church to build a new gallery and lay new floors.

Yet Allen and the black parishioners felt cramped and limited at St. George's, where they were confined to off-hours services and separate galleries. He decided that they needed a place of worship of their own. When he proposed his idea to some of the members of St. George's, only three agreed with them. But one of them was among the most determined and activist of their number.

Absalom Jones, born a slave in Sussex, Delaware, in 1746, was taken to Philadelphia by his owner when he was sixteen. He married a woman who was also his owner's slave and worked hard to purchase first his wife's freedom (so any children born to them would be automatically free) and then his own. They continued in the employ of their owner, saved their wages, and eventually bought two houses in Philadelphia, which they rented out for income. Jones was a staunch churchgoer and shared Allen's reluctance to continue as a second-class church member. The time had come for a separate black Methodist Episcopal church in Philadelphia.

The minister in charge of Methodists in Philadelphia would not hear of it. He insulted the two men and eventually barred them from meeting outside the church. Allen and Jones were in a quandary. There were not enough black Methodists to organize a powerful response. There were, however, enough black Philadelphians altogether to make their presence felt—if only they stood together. Allen and Jones decided to organize Philadelphia's blacks. In the spring of

1787, they formed the Free African Society in Philadelphia. It was primarily a self-help group, aimed especially at providing support for its members when they were sick and for widows and orphaned children.

Six months later, as Allen and Jones knelt in prayer at St. George's, they were roughly yanked from their knees by the white trustees of the church. In protest, the two men, accompanied by every other black worshiper present, left the church as a group, never to return. They were now, as Allen later recalled, "filled with fresh vigor to get a house erected to worship God in."[2] They met in a storeroom while they tried to figure out how to achieve their dream.

Allen believed that the best way to gain the support of most black Philadelphians to build a church was not to impose a specific denomination. Rather, he began to urge the building of what he called The African Church of Philadelphia that would serve a broad spectrum of beliefs. He got nowhere. Absalom Jones and most others wanted to affiliate with an established church, but there was disagreement about which one. Allen was convinced that the Methodist Church still held the most promise for blacks, but he could not persuade the others to adopt his way of thinking.

An epidemic of yellow fever raged through Philadelphia during the summer of 1793, ultimately killing 5,000 people, or about one-tenth of the population. Allen and Jones joined together to rally the city's blacks to fight the plague. Jones organized volunteers to nurse the sick and Allen the burying of the dead. Both services were performed without expectation of payment, and so it was especially insulting when the myth grew among white Philadelphians that blacks were somehow immune to the plague. Allen and Jones later published a pamphlet telling the truth about blacks and the yellow fever epidemic, asserting that "as many coloured people died in proportion as others." They further pointed out that "the burials among us have increased fourfold, was not this in a great degree the effects of the services of the unjustly vilified black people?"[3]

After the plague had ended, Philadelphia's blacks returned to the task of building a separate black church. They accomplished their goal in 1794. That summer, Absalom Jones dedicated the St. Thomas African Episcopal Church of Philadelphia. Ten years later, he would be ordained the first black priest of the Episcopal Denomination in the United States.

Still committed to the Methodist Church, Allen had gone his own way. With money earned as a master shoemaker, he purchased a lot and then an old frame building that had been a blacksmith's shop. Moving the frame to the lot, he hired carpenters to put up a church, which he named Bethel. It opened in 1794, with Allen as its deacon and elder. The following year, he established a school for sixty students in the church building. By 1810, his congregation numbered 500; by 1815, there were more black Methodists than white in Philadelphia.

Bethel became the "Mother" church of the African Methodist Episcopal (A.M.E.) Church, the first independent black denomination. Allen was the first bishop of the A.M.E. church. Inspired by Allen, black Methodists in other cities formed their own congregations. Notable among them was Peter Williams, who led black members out of the John Street Church in New York City and later established the African Methodist Episcopal Zion Church.

Allen continued to work with Jones for the benefit of the black community of Philadelphia. In 1797, they helped organize a Masonic Lodge for Pennsylvania. When British troops threatened Philadelphia during the War of 1812, the two old friends mobilized 2,500 black citizens to build defenses. Absalom Jones died in 1818; Richard Allen lived a dozen years more, actively supporting the antislavery movement, which was then gathering force. He wrote articles for *Freedom's Journal*, the country's first black newspaper, published out of New York, and presided in 1830 at the first "Convention of the People of Colour of the United States." When he died in 1831, he was widely revered both as a man of God and as a black leader.

JAMES
FORTEN

(1766–1842)

Another Philadelphian, and a contemporary of Richard Allen, was James Forten.

His father, Thomas Forten, had been freeborn and had purchased his wife's freedom with his wages as a sailmaker in the employ of Robert Bridges. James Forten was only seven when his father fell to his death while working on the tall sails of a ship. His family survived the sudden tragedy, and life went on.

James Forten attended a Quaker school as a boy. The colony of Pennsylvania had been established by the Quakers, a religious sect formally known as the Society of Friends. The Quakers believed in the equality of all people and had early on allowed blacks to attend their schools.

After the Revolutionary War, Forten became an apprentice to Robert Bridges, the Philadelphia sailmaker who had employed his father. Forten was such a skilled and responsible worker that by 1786 he had been named foreman of the sailmaking loft. Twelve years later,

THE PATRIOT

At the age of fourteen, Forten enlisted in the navy, where he served as a powder boy, loading cannons aboard the *Royal Lewis*, a privateer, or private ship commissioned by the American navy. The *Royal Lewis* was captured by the British navy, and its crew, which included some twenty blacks, were taken prisoner. Forten became friends with the British captain's son. The boy asked Forten to go back to England with him to live a life of wealth and aristocratic privilege.

Forten paused and answered, "I am a prisoner here for the liberties of my country. I never, never shall prove a traitor to her interests."[1] He was transferred to the British prison ship *Jersey* and later released in a general prisoner exchange.

in 1798, he became its owner. More than forty workers, both black and white, were employed in his factory.

Sometime after 1800, Forten invented a device that helped control the sails on ships and that opened the door to the modern sailing industry. The exact date is not known because Forten never patented his invention. He secured contracts from the United States Navy to outfit its vessels, and he quietly made a fortune.

Forten could have made even more money had he been willing to work with the slave traders. But he refused to outfit slave vessels with sail rigging or with his sail-handling device.

Forten used much of his wealth in good causes. For instance, he joined other black Philadelphia businessmen in various endeavors to help the poor. He gave a lot of money to support the *Liberator*, an antislavery newspaper founded by William Lloyd Garrison, and he helped to build its subscription list. A strong supporter of the United States government, his largest customer, he helped to recruit black soldiers to serve in the War of 1812.

Forten's friends asked him to be chairman of the Colored People's Convention, which met at Bethel Church in Philadelphia on August

10, 1817. Forten, along with 3,000 others, adopted this basic resolution: "We will never separate ourselves voluntarily from the slave population of this country; they are our brethren by ties of [shared blood], suffering and wrong; we feel there is more virtue in suffering privation with them, than fancied advantage for a reason."[2]

Forten was not in favor of colonization in Africa. "We are contented in the land that gave us birth and for which many of our fathers fought and died," he said. He had more faith in offering money to master mechanics to take black children as apprentices than in settling another country.[3]

At Forten's death in 1842, his sail loft enterprise was estimated to be worth $100,000, a vast sum for any American at that time.

DEBORAH
SAMPSON

(1760-1827)

✦

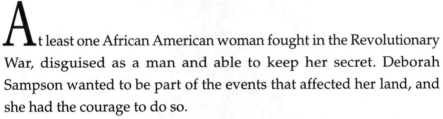

At least one African American woman fought in the Revolutionary War, disguised as a man and able to keep her secret. Deborah Sampson wanted to be part of the events that affected her land, and she had the courage to do so.

Sampson was born on December 17, 1760, in Plymouth, Massachusetts, one of several children. Her father, Jonathan Sampson, was a sailor who disappeared at sea. Her mother, unable to care for the children, sent them to different families. Five-year-old Deborah lived first with a cousin, who died when Deborah was about eight. Then Deborah spent two years with the wife of a local pastor.

At the age of ten, Sampson was sent out as a servant to Benjamin Thomas of Middleborough, Massachusetts. For eight years, she not only did domestic chores, but she also worked in the fields, cared for the farm animals, and did carpentry. In addition, she managed to attend the local public school part-time. The Thomas children taught her what they knew. An avid reader, she was especially fond of newspapers and studied the major issues of the day.

Sampson was just thirteen years old at the time of the Boston Tea Party in 1773, the first major rebellion by American colonials against Great Britain. When the colonies declared their independence and the Revolutionary War began, she could not get enough of the news.

When Sampson was eighteen years old, her bondage to the Thomas family ended. She taught for six months at the same public school that she had attended. How she made her living after that is not known. In November 1780, she joined the First Baptist Church of Middleborough, but soon encountered problems. Accused of dressing in male clothing and engaging in conduct unbecoming a respectable lady, she was banished by the congregation.[1]

Sampson chafed against the restrictions of life in that Massachusetts town when such exciting events were taking place elsewhere. At some point, she determined to volunteer for the Continental army. Sampson was above average in height for a woman. Years of hard work for the Thomas family had made her strong. She purchased fabric and sewed a man's suit for herself. Then she walked to Billingham, Massachusetts. Using the alias Robert Shurtleff (or Shirtliff or Shirtlieff), she enlisted in the Continental army. Mustered into service at Worcester, Massachusetts, on May 23, 1782, she was assigned to Captain George Webb's company in the Fourth Massachusetts Regiment.

Sampson first served at White Plains, in the colony of New York, then moved with her company to Tarrytown, New York. In the battle at Tarrytown, she was wounded three times: a sword cut on the head and two musket balls in one leg.

At the Battle of Yorktown, Pennsylvania, four months later, Sampson was shot through the shoulder. During the march north after the battle, she succumbed to the extreme cold and other deprivations suffered by the soldiers of the Continental army and collapsed.

Sampson was unconscious when she arrived at the field hospital operated by Dr. Barnabas Binney, a Philadelphia physician. In fact, it

A DARING DECEPTION

Although Deborah Sampson was seriously wounded at Tarrytown, New York, she was afraid to go to a field hospital, because her true identity might be discovered. Despite her protests, her fellow soldiers carried her six miles to the nearest hospital.

There, Sampson reported only the head wound, which she knew she could not hide. She did not mention the two musket balls in her leg. While at the hospital, she somehow managed to get hold of surgical instruments and to remove one of the musket balls herself. The other was too deep to retrieve and remained in her leg. As soon as she had recovered sufficiently, she returned to her company.

was first thought that she was dead. But Dr. Binney discerned a pulse, and in the course of treating her, he discovered that she was a woman. He kept this knowledge to himself, and when she was well enough to leave the hospital, he arranged for her to recuperate in his own home.

Formally and honorably discharged from the army by General Henry Knox at West Point on October 23, 1783, Sampson returned to New England and went to live with an uncle in Sharon, Massachusetts. There, she seems to have had no problems fitting into the community. She married a farmer named Benjamin Gannett on April 7, 1784. The couple had three children, a boy and two girls. They adopted another girl whose mother had died.

Sampson was proud of her service in the Continental army and, after her discharge, never tried to hide the truth of her daring deception. She sought, and was successful in securing, a government pension for her service. This event attracted the attention of Henry Mann, who became fascinated with her story and wrote a highly romanticized biography of Sampson, which was published in 1797. Mann also helped Sampson write a lecture about her experiences, which she first delivered at the Federal Street Theater in Boston on March 22, 1802. Thereafter, she lectured as often as she could, for her fees helped the family, who were not doing well at farming.

Sampson died on April 29, 1827, and was buried in Rockridge Cemetery in Sharon, Massachusetts. Carved on the back of her tombstone were these words: "Deborah Sampson Gannett, Robert Shurtleff, The Female Soldier: 1781–1783."

Several years later, her husband, Benjamin Gannett, petitioned Congress to collect his late wife's pension. Gannett argued that caring for her during her long and protracted illnesses resulting from her wounds in the Revolutionary War had left him in severe economic distress. In 1837, Congress granted Gannett a pension of $80 a year for the rest of his life.

A LETTER FROM PAUL REVERE

The Revolutionary War hero Paul Revere wrote a letter of support when Sampson applied for a federal government pension:

"This extraordinary woman is now in her 62d year of her age; she possesses a clear understanding, and a general knowledge of passing events; fluent in speech, and delivers her sentiment in correct language, with deliberate and measured accent; easy in deportment, affable in manners, robust . . .

"There are many living witnesses in this county, who recognized her on her appearance at the court, and were ready to attest to her services."[2]

DR. JAMES

DERHAM

(1 7 6 2 – ?)

One day in 1788, James Derham of New Orleans, Louisiana, the first black doctor in the United States, hurried through the streets of Philadelphia. He was anxious to meet Dr. Benjamin Rush, a signer of the Declaration of Independence and the foremost medical man of his day. Rush was just as eager to meet the twenty-six-year-old African American.

Although Dr. Derham had only been fourteen years old when Dr. Rush had signed the Declaration of Independence, the younger man's reputation for healing was now well known. And Dr. Rush had an urgent problem. How could he keep more people from dying in the terrible diphtheria epidemic that was sweeping the city of Philadelphia?

The epidemic had killed 119 people in Philadelphia in a single day. Physicians looked on helplessly as patients died from the dreaded disease. Rush had already lost his sister and three pupils. Doctor Derham, had developed a successful treatment for diphtheria. Benjamin Rush wanted to learn how Derham had saved so many

people. Perhaps Dr. Derham's knowledge could help him stop the diphtheria epidemic.

Like other members of the black population, Derham was struggling to make a place for himself in the new nation. He had been born in Philadelphia, but the place Derham (sometimes spelled Durham) was trying to make was unusual for anyone in those times, and especially for a black man: He was struggling for acceptance as a doctor.

Derham had been born into slavery, but he had learned to read and write. Like most doctors in this country, he had learned his profession by studying under other doctors. While still a small child, he was put to work mixing medicines by a physician who bought him from another slave owner. At age eleven, Derham was bought by yet another doctor, who taught him to perform "some of the more humble acts of attention to his patients."[1]

Finally, when he was twenty-one, the determined Derham managed to buy his freedom and begin his own medical practice in New Orleans. His fluency in French, Spanish, and English made him one of that city's most popular doctors, and he soon became one of its most distinguished ones as well.

Derham finally met Rush on that day in 1788, and gave him such good information that Rush ended up reading the young man's paper on diphtheria before the College of Physicians of Philadelphia. "I have conversed with him upon most of the acute and epidemic diseases of the country where he lives," Rush said later, "and was pleased to find him perfectly acquainted with the modern simple mode of practice in those diseases. I expected to have suggested some new medicines to him, but he suggested many more to me."[2]

Derham returned to New Orleans in 1789. There, he managed to save the lives of more yellow fever victims than most doctors of his time, losing only eleven of sixty-four patients during an epidemic that raged through the city.

Only three years later, however, the city of New Orleans limited his work because he did not have a formal medical degree. He continued to write to Dr. Rush, but today no one knows what happened to Dr. Derham after 1802. Despite his achievements, the idea that black people were incapable of understanding medicine

AFRICAN KNOW-HOW

Several decades before Rush and Derham met, the most important medical discovery in Colonial America was contributed by a black man. The man's name was Onesimus, the young African slave of the Puritan clergyman Cotton Mather.

During one of the periodic smallpox epidemics that swept the colonies, Onesimus told Mather ". . . Cut the Skin, and put in a drop . . . no body have Small Pox any more."[3] He then showed Mather the scar he had received.

Traditional healers in Africa had apparently used smallpox inoculations for centuries, injecting a mild case of the disease as a protection against a fatal attack.

Mather published the information he had received from Onesimus in *Some Account of What Is Said of Inoculating or Transplanting the Small Pox* in 1721. This was almost thirty years before Edward Jenner, the Englishman who is credited with developing the smallpox vaccine, was born. Mather was greeted with ridicule by most of the leading physicians of his time when he urged them to test the method described by Onesimus.

But a doctor named Zabdiel Boylston tried it on his son and two of his slaves during an epidemic that swept Boston that same year. When it worked on them, Boylston inoculated another 241 people. Only six later caught smallpox. (Thomas Jefferson tested a smallpox vaccine many years later by injecting it into 200 slaves, including eighty of his own. When none of them died, whites allowed themselves to be injected.)

The method Onesimus passed on to Boylston was also used to inoculate American soldiers during the Revolutionary War, saving many of them from the ravages of smallpox.

remained widespread in the decades to come. In the face of often incredible odds, however, many African American men and women wrote their names into history as outstanding doctors, nurses, and researchers.

PIERRE
TOUSSAINT

(1766–1853)

Pierre Toussaint was as successful in his time and place as Dr. James
Derham was. Toussaint was born a slave on a plantation in Haiti when
that island was a French possession prized for its sugarcane crop. A
house servant, Toussaint was encouraged to read and write and was
treated well by his owners, the wealthy and aristocratic Jean and
Marie Bérard. But the cruelty of other slaveowners led to unrest in
Haiti. The Bérards, accompanied by Toussaint, fled to New York. Fully
expecting the slave revolt in Haiti to be put down by French troops,
Jean Bérard had brought only enough money to maintain his family
comfortably in New York for one year.

Soon after settling in a rented house on Reade Street, Jean Bérard
apprenticed twenty-one-year-old Toussaint to a Mr. Merchant, one of
the city's leading hairdressers. Toussaint quickly mastered the art of
making the elaborate hairstyles that were in vogue for wealthy
women, but he had to walk to their homes to do his work, because
blacks were not allowed to ride the city's public horsecars.

The situation in Haiti grew more violent. Frightened by the rumors of impending disaster, Jean Bérard sailed to Haiti to save his property. Bérard never returned to New York; he died of pleurisy, a disease of the lungs, on his plantation. Not long after his death, his plantation was destroyed. Although French troops eventually put down the rebellion, the French hold on the island had been broken. In 1803, Haiti became an independent black republic.

Having barely adjusted to the news of Jean's death and the conditions in Haiti, Marie Bérard learned that her husband's investments in a New York City business were wiped out when the firm collapsed. Penniless, she asked Toussaint to sell some of her jewelry. He refused, offering instead to provide for the household's weekly expenses. He sometimes earned $1,000 per year per client at a time when a man was considered wealthy if he made $10,000 a year.

Although he had every right to be free, Toussaint was sensitive to Madame Bérard's feelings and to appearances, and he always acted the dutiful slave. Marie Bérard remarried, but her new husband, Gabriel Nicolas, also a refugee French planter from Haiti, suffered financial reverses. Pierre Toussaint continued to support the household. In fact, he put off his own plans to marry a young Haitian girl, Juliette Nöel, because he felt that he could not marry her while he was responsible for the Nicolas family.

Marie Nicolas died when Toussaint was forty-five years old. On her deathbed, she informed him that she had provided for his freedom in a legal document dated July 2, 1807.

Pierre Toussaint wasted no time in marrying Juliette, but otherwise he continued to live much as he always had, attending early mass each morning before he went to work. He used his money to help the poor. He provided much of the support for the Prince Street Orphanage, New York's first Catholic institution for homeless children, and he helped raise funds to build St. Patrick's Cathedral and St. Vincent de Paul Church.

Pierre and Juliette took orphans into their home. Toussaint also put his life on the line to nurse victims of cholera and yellow fever, crossing quarantine barriers to reach sufferers in the city's early ghettoes. He continued to work well into his later years. One of his customers said, "Toussaint, you are the richest man I know. Why not stop working?" Toussaint replied, "Then, Madame, I should not have enough for others."[1] He continued to work until Juliette died in 1851. Not long afterward, Toussaint himself became ill. He died on June 30, 1853, at the age of eighty-seven.

Pierre Toussaint was first buried in the cemetery of Old St. Patrick's Church on Mott Street. His remains now lie in a crypt beneath the floor of St. Patrick's Cathedral on Fifth Avenue in New York City. Catholic church officials had come to believe that the good man they reburied there was very likely a saint.

"FREE FRANK"
McWORTER

(1777–1854)

Frank McWorter built an entire town in the pursuit of complete freedom for his family. He was born a slave in Union County, South Carolina, a frontier outpost. His mother, Juda, had been born in western Africa. Evidence indicates that Juda's owner, George McWhorter, was Frank's father.

Around 1795, George McWhorter purchased land in Pulaski County, Kentucky, some two hundred miles northwest of Union County, South Carolina. Kentucky law stated that in order to own the land, the buyer must live on it, fence two acres, and cultivate a crop of corn. So George McWhorter sent eighteen-year-old Frank and three other McWhorter slaves to Kentucky to establish his claim to the land.

During that year in Kentucky, Frank met Lucy, who belonged to William Denham, a relative of the McWhorters. Four years later Frank and Lucy chose to be man and wife, although slaves in Kentucky were not allowed to marry. Because their respective masters lived some distance away from each other, Frank and Lucy were unable to live together under a single roof. Over the course of the next eighteen

years, however, they had thirteen children, all of them the legal property of Lucy's owner.

The years passed. They were hard but never boring. Frank got George McWhorter's permission to hire out his own time as a jack-of-all-trades, agreeing to pay an annual fee for the privilege. After George moved his family south to Wayne County and left Frank in charge of the Pulaski County farm, Frank had even more time to work for himself. But it was the War of 1812 that led him to establish his own business.

In its fight against Great Britain, the United States needed huge quantities of saltpeter, the principal ingredient in gunpowder. Kentucky was the nation's leading producer of saltpeter, and the Rockcastle caves, rich in potassium nitrate, or niter, saltpeter's basic ingredient, were only a short distance away from the McWhorter farm in Pulaski County. Frank worked the farm by day and devoted his nights to mining and producing saltpeter. After the War of 1812, as the demand for saltpeter declined, Frank also went into the business of making salt. In those days, salt-making even on a small scale could be profitable.

George McWhorter died in 1815. Before his death, he had promised to free Frank, but he had made no provision in his will for Frank's emancipation. McWhorter's heirs agreed to free Frank, on payment of $500, more money than Frank had yet saved. That year, Lucy gave birth to their thirteenth child, Solomon. By 1817, she was pregnant again. Frank did not want his fourteenth child born in slavery, and by then he had earned enough to buy Lucy's freedom. He purchased her for $800. As a consequence, their child, Squire, born the following September, was the first member of their family to be born free.

In 1819, Frank purchased himself, paying $800. His owners had decided to raise his price! Rather than choose a surname, he proudly had his name listed as Free Frank in the 1820 census. From then on, Frank paid whatever price freedom demanded.

Ten years later, in 1829, Free Frank purchased freedom for his twenty-five-year-old son, Frank Junior, by trading his saltpeter works to the Denham family. Three years earlier, young Frank had escaped and made it safely to Canada. But Free Frank wanted his son with him, and so he bought his freedom in his absence.

Now that Free Frank had traded away his main source of income, he had little reason to stay in Kentucky. It was no longer a frontier. In 1830, he sold the land he had acquired and moved the free members of his family—Frank Junior and Squire, Commodore, and Lucy Ann, three children who had been born free after 1817—to Illinois, a free state. They traveled by ox-drawn wagon, crossed the Ohio River on a flatboat, and settled in Hadley Township in Pike County, on the Illinois frontier.

By the time they reached Illinois, Free Frank and his family had dropped the "h" in their last name and were known as the McWorters. The family, who at the time were the only blacks in Pike County, bought land and began to raise hogs and horses for cash money to buy Frank and Lucy's children who remained in slavery.

Four years later, in 1835, Frank purchased his son Solomon for $550. Two daughters and their children remained in slavery. (Frank and Lucy's other slave children had died by this time.) Money was scarce, and time seemed to be running out.

Then Free Frank had his best moneymaking idea yet. He decided to establish a town, primarily because selling lots was the best way to obtain cash money. He bought land and had it surveyed, or plotted. He named the town New Philadelphia. Free Frank was a deeply religious man, and it is possible that he took the name from a passage in Revelation, in which God says: "To the angel of the church in Philadelphia. . . . I know your deeds; that is why I have left before you an open door which no one can close."[1]

New Philadelphia was one of six towns founded by single proprietors in Pike County at that time. Free Frank quickly opened a store

Trying to get ahead, thousands of African Americans like the McWorters headed to the next frontier to earn money, their freedom, or both. Most became merchants, farmers, or cowboys. During the 1849 Gold Rush, some like this miner went all the way to California to seek their fortune.

and worked with county officials to build cross-county roads nearby. He had sold eight town lots by 1841; the purchasers included whites. With the increased prosperity of the county in the middle 1840s, New Philadelphia grew. Soon it had a stagecoach stop and a post office.

By 1850, Free Frank and his family owned over 600 acres of land valued at more than $7,000. Only 3,000 of the nation's nearly 440,000 free blacks owned land. In that year, Free Frank purchased two of his grandchildren and the wife of his son Squire. By 1854, he had purchased four more family members.

Free Frank McWorter died on September 7, 1854, at the age of seventy-seven. He had not lived to accomplish his dream of freeing his entire family, but his will provided for his work to go on. His sons carried out his wishes, and within three years they purchased a total of seven more grandchildren and great-grandchildren. Altogether, fifteen members of the Frank McWorter family were freed from bondage, at a cost of more than $14,000.

CATHERINE (KATY)
FERGUSON

(C. 1779–1854)

Catherine Williams was born into slavery on a schooner sailing to New York City. At the time of her birth, her mother was being transported from Virginia to a new slave owner. Catherine, who would become known as Katy, was only eight years old when her mother was again sold. Katy never saw her again. The pain this separation caused may have been the reason she spent her adult life helping motherless children.

Katy was a deeply religious child. Though her mother could not read or write, she had taught Katy the Scriptures. And although Katy was a slave, she was allowed to attend New York City's Associate Reformed Church on Murray Street.

At age ten, Katy promised her owner that if he gave her freedom, she would serve the Lord forever. Her owner, a Presbyterian elder, denied her request and continued to hold her in bondage. When Katy was sixteen, however, a sympathetic woman purchased her freedom for $200. Katy earned her living as a professional cake-maker for weddings and parties.

Katy's lifelong mission of helping poor children began four years later. Soon after her emancipation, she met and married a man named Ferguson and they had two children. Both children died in infancy, and her husband passed away before she was twenty. She never mentioned him again to friends or acquaintances. Instead, from that time on, she poured her heart into teaching and helping others.

Catherine Ferguson began helping the destitute children she saw near her home in lower Manhattan. There was little provision for educating the poor in the late eighteenth and early nineteenth centuries. Some were able to learn the rudiments of reading and writing by studying the Bible, and this is how Catherine began to teach her charges. Every Sunday, Ferguson "regularly collected the children in the neighborhood who are accustomed to run in the street on the Lord's day, into her house and got suitable persons to come and hear them say their catechism . . ."[1]

Ferguson supported her school with the money she earned from catering, and from her skill at cleaning fine laces. Sometime around 1814, the Reverend John Mitchell Mason of the Murray Street church invited her to relocate her activities to the church's lecture room. Katy accepted the offer, and from then on her school was known as the Murray Street Sabbath School. It was one of the earliest Sunday schools in New York City.

She continued to teach the Scriptures, while Reverend Mason provided her with assistants who taught the regular school subjects. The Sabbath School report for 1818—the only one that survives— shows that the school had eighty-eight students: twenty-six black and sixty-two white. Eleven of the black students were adults.

Ferguson also took both black and white homeless children into her own household, often going to the almshouses to seek them out. Some of the girls were unwed mothers. Treated as social outcasts, these girls had no place to go either during their pregnancies or after giving birth. Ferguson's organized effort was the first to help unwed mothers in New York City, and perhaps the first in the nation. A newspaper article published shortly after her death estimated that she had cared for twenty black and twenty-eight white children from the almshouses or from destitute parents.

Catherine Ferguson died of cholera in New York City on July 11, 1854. She was about seventy-five years old. Her efforts had become so widely known that an obituary was carried in the *New York Times,* and a short biographical article was published in the *New York Daily Tribune.*

She had spent the major part of her life serving poor people, especially the young, giving unknown numbers of them an education they would never have received otherwise. Her love and compassion also rescued scores from a life without hope.

In 1920, Ferguson's pioneering work as an educator and social worker was recognized when the Katy Ferguson Home for Unwed Mothers was opened in New York City. It was said to be the only home of its kind for black women in the United States.

In that same year, famed scholar W. E. B. Du Bois praised her in a collection of essays titled *Darkwater: Voices from Within the Veil,* as an example of that "human sympathy and sacrifice . . . characteristic of Negro womanhood."[2]

In words that summed up her labors of a lifetime and the love she had so freely given, Du Bois wrote that Catherine (Katy) Ferguson had taken "the children of the streets of New York, white and black, to her empty arms, taught them, [and] found them homes. . . ."[3]

DANIEL
COKER

(1780–1846)

Daniel Coker, like Paul Cuffe before him, came to the conclusion that blacks could never be truly free in the new United States of America. Born a slave in Baltimore County, Maryland, to a black father and an indentured white mother, Coker became a fighter for African American freedom.

Daniel was raised with his white half-brothers, who were children of his mother's first marriage. He accompanied them to school as their servant. Quietly, he listened to the teachers' lessons. He could not be a regular student because it was illegal for anyone to educate a slave. But Daniel longed for education and freedom. He escaped to New York City while still a youth. There, he managed to obtain a good education, which was rare for an American of any color in that era. In addition, he was ordained a Methodist minister.

Now he was ready to return to Baltimore. But the move would have to be made in great secrecy because he was legally still a slave. He could be returned to slavery at any time, so going home was dangerous. Friends, however, soon raised enough money to help him

buy his freedom. At this time, the Constitution of the United States protected slavery and declared that African Americans were only three-fifths of a human being.

Courageous and passionate, Coker ignored the dangers and began speaking out boldly against slavery and the treatment of black people throughout the United States. His fight for black freedom would last for the rest of his life. Like Benjamin Banneker, Coker would publish pamphlets to denounce slavery. One in particular, *A Dialogue*

SCHOOLS OF OUR OWN: THE PRINCE HALL STORY

In the early years, free African Americans had to start their own schools. Both blacks and whites in colonial America knew that educated people would struggle constantly to end slavery. For that reason, the education of slaves was banned almost everywhere, and the education of free black people was strongly discouraged.

The small free black population repeatedly demanded that their children be educated. In 1787, Prince Hall and several other African American parents wrote to the Massachusetts state legislature. They petitioned for "the education of our children which now receive no benefit from the free schools in the town of Boston, which we think is a great grievance, as by woeful experience we now feel the want of a common education. . . . We therefore pray your Honors that you would in your wisdom [make] some provision, . . . for the education of our dear children. . . ."[1] The legislators ignored Hall's request, so he helped establish a school in his own home and he hired two Harvard students as teachers.

The next year, Hall helped a black Baptist minister start a school for the children in his congregation, raising the necessary money from the contributions of black seamen along Boston's waterfront.

Free African Americans in other states also established schools. One was organized in Philadelphia by the Society of Free People of Color for Promoting the Instruction and School Education of Children of African Descent.

Between a Virginian and an African Minister (1810), became popular because it used arguments from the Bible.

In 1802, Coker began teaching in the African School conducted by the Sharp Street Church in Baltimore. He taught there for the next fourteen years, combining his teaching with denunciations of slavery.

During those years at the Sharp Street Church, Coker and several other church leaders argued for the establishment of independent African Methodist churches. One of those leaders was Richard Allen, who had formed the first African Methodist Episcopal congregation several years earlier. In April 1816, Allen invited Coker and fourteen other Methodist leaders to a meeting in Philadelphia.

On April 9, 1816, these leaders and ministers formed a national organization called the African Methodist Episcopal Church. They elected Coker as their first bishop, but he declined the honor, which then went to Allen. When the African Methodist Episcopal Church in Baltimore established the African Bethel School, they turned to Coker

Eager young students filled the newly created Baltimore Freedmen School.

again for help. This time he said yes. He spent the next four years as the school's teacher and manager.

In 1820, however, a new adventure captured the teacher's imagination. He became a missionary for the Maryland Colonization Society. The goal of colonization societies was to resettle free African Americans in other lands, especially Africa. Most black leaders thought the colonization schemes were a way to protect slavery and rid the United States of free black people. But some black Americans, including Coker, supported colonization because they believed whites would never treat them with dignity and equality in this country. So it was that Daniel Coker boarded a crowded ship bound for Africa. Coker kept a daily account of his voyage. He called it the *Journal of Daniel Coker, a Descendant of Africa, from the time of Leaving New York in the Ship Elizabeth, . . . on a Voyage for Sherbro, in Africa, in Company with Three Agents and about Ninety Persons of Colour . . . With an Appendix.*

Unfortunately, the three agents who accompanied the colonists soon died, leaving Coker with the sole responsibility of trying to establish a colony. He persevered and was commended by the managers of the colonization society for his "care, attention, and prudence, . . . in a time of great difficulty, and danger."[2]

Coker spent the rest of his life in Africa. He died in Freetown, Sierra Leone, leaving behind the church he had built on that African soil.

CHRONOLOGY

1502   First enslaved Africans to arrive in the New World land in Hispaniola (now Haiti and the Dominican Republic)

1503   Estevanico (Stephan Dorantez) born

1513   Estevanico is among thirty Africans who accompany the explorer Balboa, the first European to see the eastern coast of the Pacific Ocean

1522   First slave revolt takes place in Hispaniola

1536   Estevanico explores Mexico

1539   Estevanico dies

1613   Free black sailor Jan Rodriguez arrives on Manhattan Island to trade with Native Americans for the Dutch

1619   First Africans arrive in British North American colonies, sold as laborers in Jamestown, Virginia

1621   Anthony Johnson sold into slavery in Jamestown

1624   First black child born in British North America in Jamestown

1651   Anthony Johnson, freed, receives a land grant of 250 acres

1670   Anthony Johnson dies

1676   Native Americans lose their war against the British called "Prince Philip's War"

1700   Enslaved population in British North America is 27,817, of which 22,600 are in the Southern colonies

1723   Crispus Attucks born

1731   Benjamin Banneker born

1742   Marie-Thérèse Metoyer (Coincoin) born

1745   Jean Baptiste Point du Sable born

1750   Peter Salem born

1753   Phillis Wheatley born

        Lemuel Haynes born

1759   Paul Cuffe born

1760   Deborah Sampson born

        Richard Allen born

1761   Enslaved population in America is 230,000, still mostly in the South

1762   France cedes the Louisiana Purchase to Spain

        Dr. James Derham born

1766	James Forten born
	Pierre Toussaint born
1770	Crispus Attucks dies in the Boston Massacre
1773	Phillis Wheatley's *Poems on Various Subjects, Religious and Moral,* is the first book written by a black in North America and the second by a woman
1775	Battles of Lexington and Concord
	Battle of Bunker Hill
	First abolition society formed in Philadelphia
1776	The Revolutionary War begins
	The Declaration of Independence issued
1777	Free Frank McWorter born
1779	Catherine (Katy) Ferguson born
1780	Daniel Coker born
1783	The Revolutionary War ends
1784	Phillis Wheatley dies
	Jean Baptiste Point du Sable founds a trading post that will become the city of Chicago
1792	Benjamin Banneker publishes his first almanac
1803	Haiti becomes an independent black republic
1806	Benjamin Banneker dies
1812	War of 1812
1816	Marie-Thérèse Metoyer (Coincoin) dies
	Private Peter Salem dies
1817	Paul Cuffe dies
1818	Jean Baptiste Point du Sable dies
1831	Richard Allen dies
1833	Lemuel Haynes dies
1842	James Forten dies
1846	Daniel Coker dies
1847	Deborah Sampson dies
1854	Catherine (Katy) Ferguson dies
	Free Frank McWorter dies
1861	The Civil War begins

NOTES

BENJAMIN BANNEKER

1. Rev. William J. Simmons, *Men of Mark, Progressive and Rising* (New York: Arno Press and The New York Times Company, 1968), 344.
2. Silvio A. Bedini, *The Life of Benjamin Banneker* (New York: Charles Scribner's Sons, 1972), 40.
3. Ibid., 122.
4. Ibid., 153.
5. Sidney Kaplan and Emma Nogrady Kaplan, *The Black Presence in the Era of the American Revolution* (Amherst: University of Massachusetts Press, 1989), 145.

PRIVATE PETER SALEM

1. Sidney Kaplan, *The Black Presence in the Era of the American Revolution, 1770-1800* (Washington, D.C.: Smithsonian Institution, 1973), 18.

PRIVATE AUSTIN DABNEY

1. Sidney Kaplan, *The Black Presence in the Era of the American Revolution, 1770–1800* (Washington, D.C.: Smithsonian Institution, 1973), 52.

PRIVATE LEMUEL HAYNES

1. Sidney Kaplan, *The Black Presence in the Era of the American Revolution, 1770–1800* (Washington, D.C.: Smithsonian Institution, 1973), 103.
2. Ibid.
3. Robert Ewell Greene, *Black Defenders of America 1775–1973* (Chicago: Johnson Publishing, 1974), 13.
4. Kaplan, 105.

PAUL CUFFE

1. Sidney Kaplan, *The Black Presence in the Era of the American Revolution, 1770–1800* (Washington, D.C.: Smithsonian Institution, 1973), 134.
2. Ibid., 133.
3. Ibid., 138–140.

RICHARD ALLEN

1. Sidney Kaplan, *The Black Presence in the Era of the American Revolution 1770–1800* (Washington, D.C.: Smithsonian Institution Press, 1973), 82.
2. Ibid., p. 85.
3. Ibid., p. 87.

JAMES FORTEN

1. Harry S. Ploski and James Williams, eds., *The Negro Almanac: A Reference Work on the Afro-American* (New York: John Wiley & Sons, 1983), 804.
2. Mabel M. Smythe, ed., *The Black American Reference Book* (Englewood Cliffs, N.J.: Prentice-Hall, 1976), 543.
3. Dorothy Sterling, ed., *Speak Out in Thunder Tones: Letters and Other Writings by Black Northerners, 1787–1865* (Garden City, N.Y.: Doubleday, 1973), 59.

DEBORAH SAMPSON

1. Jessie Carney Smith, ed., *Epic Lives: One Hundred Black Women Who Made A Difference* (Detroit: Visible Ink Press, 1993), 974.
2. Ibid., 975.

DR. JAMES DERHAM

1. Herbert Morais, *The History of the Afro-American in Medicine* (Cornwells Heights, PA: Publishers Agency, 1976), 8.

PIERRE TOUSSAINT

1. "The Quiet Man," *The Anthonian* (June 27, 1976), 4–31.

"FREE FRANK" MCWORTER

1. King James Version of the Bible, Revelation 3:7–8

CATHERINE (KATY) FERGUSON

1. "Catherine Ferguson, Black Founder of a Sunday-School," *Negro History Bulletin* (December 1972), 176.
2. Walter Wilson, ed., *The Selected Writings of W.E.B. Du Bois* (New York: A Mentor Book, 1970), 97.
3. Ibid., 97.

DANIEL COKER

1. Sidney Kaplan and Emma Nogrady Kaplan, *The Black Presence in the Era of the American Revolution* (Amherst: University of Massachusetts Press, 1989), 209.
2. Rayford W. Logan and Michael R. Winston, eds., *Dictionary of American Negro Biography* (New York: W. W. Norton & Company, 1982), 120.

BIBLIOGRAPHY

BOOKS

Adams, Russell L. *Great Negroes Past and Present.* Chicago: Afro-Am Publishing Co., 1984.

Allen, Anne B. "Estevanico, The Moor," *American History* (August 1997).

Bedini, Silvio A. *The Life of Benjamin Banneker.* New York: Charles Scribner's Sons, 1972.

Bell, Roseann P., Bettye J. Parker, Patricia Bell Scott, and Beverly Guy-Shaftall. *Sturdy Black Bridges.* New York: Doubleday, 1979.

Busby, Margaret. *Daughters of Africa.* New York: Ballantine Books, 1992.

Donelson, Kenneth L. and Alleen Pace Nilsen. *Literature for Today's Young Adults.* Glenview, Ill.: Scott, Foresman & Company, 1980.

Franklin, John Hope, and August Meir, eds. *Black Leaders of the Twentieth Century.* Urbana: University of Illinois Press, 1982.

Gates, Henry Louis Jr. and Nellie Y. McKay, eds. *The Norton Anthology of African American Literature.* New York: W. W. Norton & Company, 1977.

Giddings, Paula. *When and Where I Enter: The Impact of Black Women on Race and Sex in America.* New York: William Morrow & Company, 1984.

Greene, Robert Ewell. *Black Defenders of America 1775–1973.* Chicago: Johnson Publishing, 1974.

Harley, Sharon. *The Timetables of African American History: A Chronology of the Most Important People and Events in African American History.* New York: Touchstone/Simon & Schuster, 1996.

Haskins, Jim. *Against All Opposition: Black Explorers in America.* New York: Walker and Company, 1992.

Haskins, Jim. *One More River to Cross: The Stories of Twelve Black Americans.* New York: Scholastic, Inc., 1992.

Hull, Gloria T., Patricia Bell Scott, and Barbara Smith. *But Some of Us Are Brave.* New York: Feminist Press, 1982.

Kaplan, Sidney. *The Black Presence in the Era of the American Revolution 1770–1800.* Washington, D.C.: Smithsonian Institution, 1973.

Kaplan, Sidney, and Emma Nogrady Kaplan. *The Black Presence in the Era of the Revolution.* Amherst: University of Massachusetts Press, 1989.

Lanker, Brian, Barbara Sumners, and Yvonne Easton. *I Dream a World: Portraits of Black Women Who Changed America.* New York: Stewart, Tabori & Chang, 1989.

Lerner, Gerda, ed. *Black Women in White America: A Documentary History.* New York: Vintage/Random House, 1972.

Littlefield, Daniel C. *Revolutionary Citizens: African Americans 1776–1804.* New York: Oxford University Press, 1997.

Logan, Rayford W. and Michael R. Winston, eds. *Dictionary of American Negro Biography.* New York: W.W. Norton & Company, 1982.

Morais, Herbert. *The History of the Afro-American in Medicine.* Cornwells Heights, PA: Publishers Agency, 1976.

Noble, Jean. *Beautiful Also Are the Souls of My Sisters: A History of the Black Woman in America.* Englewood Cliffs, N.J.: Prentice-Hall, 1978.

Ploski, Harry S. and James Williams, eds. *The Negro Almanac: A Reference Work on the Afro-American.* New York: John Wiley & Sons, 1983.

Richmond, Merle. *Phillis Wheatley: American Women of Achievement.* New York: Chelsea House, 1988.

Simmons, Rev. William J. *Men of Mark, Progressive and Rising.* New York: Arno Press and The New York Times Company, 1968.

Smith, Jessie Carney, ed. *Epic Lives: One Hundred Black Women Who Made A Difference.* Detroit: Visible Ink Press, 1993.

Smythe, Mabel M., ed. *The Black American Reference Book.* Englewood Cliffs, N.J.: Prentice-Hall, 1976.

Sterling, Dorothy, ed. *Speak Out in Thunder Tones: Letters and Other Writings by Black Northerners, 1787–1865.* Garden City, N.Y.: Doubleday, 1973.

Tate, Claudia. *Black Women Writers at Work.* New York: Continuum, 1984.

Wade-Gayes, Gloria. *No Crystal Stair: Visions of Race and Gender in Black Women's Fiction.* Cleveland: The Pilgrim Press, 1997.

Walker, Margaret. *On Being Female, Black, and Free: Essays.* Knoxville: University of Tennessee Press, 1998.

Washington, Mary Helen, ed. *Black-Eyed Susans and Midnight Birds: Stories by and about Black Women.* New York: Anchor/Doubleday, 1990 (originally published 1975 & 1980).

Wilson, Walter, ed. *The Selected Writings of W.E.B. Du Bois.* New York: A Mentor Book, 1970.

————, ed. *Invented Lives: Narratives of Black Women (1860–1960).* New York: Anchor/Doubleday, 1987.

ARTICLES

"The Quiet Man," *The Anthonian* (June 27, 1976).

"Catherine Ferguson, Black Founder of a Sunday-School," *Negro History Bulletin* (December 1972).

PICTURE CREDITS

Page 4: courtesy of the New York Public Library; page 10: courtesy of The Library of Virginia; page 14: courtesy of Corbis; pages 19 and 23: courtesy of the Library of Congress, Washington, D.C.; page 25: from Geoffrey Williams, African Designs from Traditional Sources (New York: Dover, 1971), 113; page 27: courtesy of the Library of Congress, Washington, D.C.; page 30: courtesy of the Chicago Historical Society; page 36: courtesy of the Yale University Art Gallery, New Haven, Conn.; page 40: courtesy of the Library of Congress, Washington, D.C.; page 41: courtesy of the Virginia Historical Society, Richmond; page 43: courtesy of Culver Pictures, Inc.; page 50: Museum of Art/Rhode Island School of Design, Providence; page 55: courtesy of Old Dartmouth Historical Society-New Bedford (Mass.); page 60: courtesy of Corbis; page 66: courtesy of the Historical Society of Pennsylvania/Leon Gardiner Collection; page 70: public domain; page 75: courtesy of the Library of Congress, Washington, D.C.; page 80: collection of the New York Historical Society; page 87: courtesy of the DuSable Museum of African American History, Chicago; page 90: courtesy of Photographs and Print Division, Schomburg Center for Research in Black Culture, the New York Public Library/Astor, Lenox and Tilden Foundations; page 94: courtesy of Association for the Study of African American Life and History, Silver Spring, Md.; page 96: courtesy of Photographs and Print Division, Schomburg Center for Research in Black Culture, the New York Public Library/Astor, Lenox and Tilden Foundations.

Author Credits

KEY:

Entrepreneurs: Jim Haskins, *African American Entrepreneurs* (New York: John Wiley & Sons, Inc., 1998).

Military Heroes: Jim Haskins, *African American Military Heroes* (New York: John Wiley & Sons, Inc. 1998).

Teachers: Clinton Cox, *African American Teachers* (New York: John Wiley & Sons, Inc., 2000).

Writers: Brenda Wilkinson, *African American Women Writers* (New York: John Wiley & Sons, Inc., 2000).

BY JIM HASKINS:

Estevanico; Anthony Johnson; Crispus Attucks; Marie-Thérèse Metoyer, adapted from *Entrepreneurs;* John Baptiste Point du Sable; Private Peter Salem, adapted from *Military Heroes;* Private Austin Dabney, adapted from *Military Heroes;* Private Lemuel Haynes, adapted from *Military Heroes;* Paul Cuffe, adapted from *Entrepreneurs;* Richard Allen; James Forten, adapted from *Entrepreneurs;* Deborah Sampson, adapted from *Military Heroes;* Pierre Toussaint, adapted from *Entrepreneurs;* "Free Frank" McWorter, adapted from *Entrepreneurs.*

BY CLINTON COX:

Benjamin Banneker, adapted from *Teachers;* Dr. James Derham, adapted from *Healers;* Catherine (Katy) Ferguson, adapted from *Teachers;* Daniel Coker, adapted from *Teachers.*

BY BRENDA WILKINSON:

Phillis Wheatley, adapted from *Writers.*

INDEX

Adams, John, 16, 17
African Bethel School, 96–97
African Church of Philadelphia, The, 63
African Methodist Episcopal (A.M.E.) Church, 64, 96
African Methodist Episcopal Zion Church, 64
African nation for black emigrants from America, supporters of, 58, 68, 97
Allen, Ethan, 51
Allen, Richard, 59–64, 96
almanacs, 22–23
Alpha (ship), 57–58
Armistead, James, 41
Asbury, Francis, 61
astronomers, 21, 22
Attucks, Crispus, 13–17
Attucks, John, 15

Balboa, Vasco Nuñez de, 3
Ball, Captain Lebbeus, 51
Banneker, Benjamin, 18–23
Battle Creek, Battle of, 39
Benjamin Banneker's Pennsylvania, Delaware, Maryland and Virginia Almanack and Ephemeris . . ., 22–23
Bérard, Jean and Marie, 79–81
Binney, Dr. Barnabas, 71–72
Boston Massacre, 16
Boylston, Zabdiel, 77
Bridges, Robert, 65
Bunker Hill, Battle of, 35–37

Cabeza de Vaca, Alvar Nuñez, 5–7

Castillo, Alonso, 5–7
Chew, Benjamin, 59
Chicago, Illinois, 33–34
chronology, 99–100
churches, black, 59–64, 96
Clemorgan, Jacques, 29, 31–32, 33
Coincoin, 24–28
Coker, Daniel, 93–97
Colored People's Convention of 1817, 67–68
Condorcet, Marquis de, 23
Convention of the People of Colour of the United States, 64
Cooley, Timothy, 52
Cuffe, Alice Pequit, 56
Cuffe, John, 56, 57
Cuffe, Paul, 54–58

Dabney, Austin, 39–41
Darkwater: Voices from Within the Veil (Du Bois), 92
Daughters of the American Revolution, 38
Derais, Michael, 33
Derham, Dr. James, 74–78
Dialogue Between a Virginian and an African Minister, A, 95–96
diphtheria, 74–76
doctors, 74–78
Dorantes, Andres de, 5–7
Du Bois, W. E. B., 92
Du Sable, Catherine, 32, 33
Du Sable, Jean Baptiste Point, 29–34
Du Sable, Suzanne, 32, 33

Edgel, Captain Simon, 35

education, 96
  assumptions about capabilities of
    blacks to learn, 18, 23, 46
  of free blacks, 20, 21, 56, 95
  of slaves, 2, 44, 49–51, 69, 76, 79,
    90, 93, 95
educators, 18–23, 71, 91, 95, 96–97
Ellicott, Major Andrew, 22
Ellicott, George, 21
entrepreneurs, 24–28, 29–34, 65–68
Estevanico (Stephan Dorantez), 3–8
explorers, 1, 3–8

Ferguson, Catherine (Katy), 89–92
Fitch, Eunice, 45
Fitch, Timothy, 42
Forten, James, 65–68
Franklin, Benjamin, 46
Free African Society, 63
Freedman's Bank of Boston, 38
freedom from slavery:
  purchasing, 2, 9, 26–28, 56, 61, 65,
    76, 83–88, 90, 95
  running away to achieve, 2, 9,
    13–15, 93
Freedom's Journal, 64
French and Indian Wars, 31

Gannett, Benjamin, 72, 73
Garrison, William Lloyd, 67
George III, King of England, 15, 17
Georgetown Weekly Ledger, 22
Georgia Assembly, 41
Gold Rush of 1849, 87
Grosvenor, Lieutenant, 37
Gwinn, Captain Peter, 42

Haiti, 79–81
Hall, Jacob, 21
Hall, Prince, 95
Hancock, John, 45

Harris (white soldier), 39, 41
Hawikuh, 7, 8
Haynes, Elizabeth Babbitt, 52
Haynes, Lemuel, 49–53
Hutchins, Thomas, 45
Hutchinson, Thomas, 17

indentured servants, 9, 20, 93
Indians, American, 5, 9, 31, 32, 56
inventors, 67
Isle Brevelle, 26, 27, 28

Jamaica, 38
Jefferson, Thomas, 22, 77
Johnson, Anthony, 9–12
Johnson, Mary, 9, 11
Johnson, Richard, 11, 12
Jones, Absalom, 62–63, 64
Journal of Daniel Coker . . ., 97

Katy Ferguson Home for Unwed
  Mothers, 92
King Philip's War, 15
Kinzie, John, 33
Knox, General Henry, 72

Lafayette, Marquis de, 41
Lalime, John, 33
Lexington and Concord, Battles of,
  17, 35, 51
Liberator, 67
Liberia, 58
L'Ouverture, Touissant, 38

McWorter, "Free Frank," 83–88
McWorter, Lucy, 83–85
Mann, Henry, 72–73
Maroons, 38
Maryland Colonization Society, 97
Mary (schooner), 57
Mason, Reverend John Mitchell, 91

Mather, Cotton, 77

medicine, African Americans in, 74–78

Methodism, 59–64, 93

Metoyer, Claude-Thomas-Pierre, 26

Metoyer, Marie-Thérère, 24–28

Middlebury College, 53

ministers, 51, 52, 61–64, 93

Moses, Ruth, 56

Murray Street Sabbath School, 91

Narváez, Pánfilo de, 5

National Historic Landmarks, 28, 58

Nell, William C., 37

New Philadelphia, 86–88

Nicolas, Gabriel, 81

Niza, Fray Marcos de, 7

Onesimus, 77

"On the Arrival of the Ships of War, and Landing of the Troops," 45

Peters, John, 47

Phillis, 42

Pitcairn, Major John, 35, 37

Poems on Various Subjects, Religious and Moral, by Phillis Wheatley, Negro Servant to Mrs. Wheatley of Boston, 46

poets, 42–48

poor children, helping of, 81–82, 91–92

Preston, Captain, 16

Prince Street Orphanage, 81

Quakers, 65

Quetzalcoatl, 6

Ranger (ship), 54, 57

Revere, Paul, 73

Revolutionary War, 15–17, 32–33

African Americans fighting in, 2, 13, 16–17, 35–38, 39–41, 51, 69–73

African American undercover agent in, 41

female African American fighting in, 69–73

Rose, Deacon David, 49–51

Royal Lewis (ship), 67

Rush, Dr. Benjamin, 74–76, 77

Saint-Denis, Marie de, 24, 26

St. Domingue, 38

St. George's Methodist Episcopal Church, 61–62, 63

St. Patrick's Cathedral, 81, 82

St. Thomas African Episcopal Church of Philadelphia, 64

St. Vincent de Paul Church, 81

Salem, Katie Benson, 37

Salem, Peter, 35–38

Sampson, Deborah, 69–73

Scarburgh, Edmund, 11, 12

Seven Cities of Gold, 7

shipowners, 54–58

Sierra Leone, 58, 97

slaveowners, black, 2, 9–11, 26

slavery, African:

differences within the colonies, 1–2, 24

establishment in the colonies, 1

fighters for freedom from, 93–97

freedom from, *see* freedom from slavery

legal system in the colonies and, 11, 12

slave trade, 27, 31, 42, 44, 67, 90

Slocum, Cuffe, 56

smallpox inoculations, 77

Society of Free People of Color for Promoting the Instruction and School Education of Children of African Descent, 95

stamps honoring African Americans, 34, 35, 38

Sturgis, Stokeley, 59–61

surveyors, 21–22

Suzanne (ship), 31

Tanner, Obour, 45

Tarrytown, Battle at, 71, 72

Thomas, Benjamin, 69

Ticonderoga, Fort, 51

Tonies Vineyard, 11–12

Touissant, Juliette Nöel, 81–82

Touissant, Pierre, 79–82

Trumbull, John, 37, 38

U.S. Navy, 67

unwed mothers, helping of, 91–92

Upson, Stephen, 41

Wainer, Michael, 57

War of 1812, 64, 67, 85

War of Independence, *see* Revolutionary War

Washington, D.C., surveyors of, 21–22

Washington, George, 22, 47

Webb, Captain George, 71

Welsh, Molly, 20

Wheatley, Mary, 44, 45

Wheatley, Nathaniel, 44, 46

Wheatley, Phillis, 42–48

Wheatley, Susannah and John, 44, 46

Whitefield, Reverend, George, 45

Williams, Peter, 64

yellow fever, 63

Yorktown, Battle of, 71

Zuñis, 7, 8